PHASES OF MODERN MUSIC

PHASES OF MODERN MUSIC

STRAUSS—MAC DOWELL—ELGAR—LOEFFLER
MASCAGNI—GRIEG—CORNELIUS—VERDI
—WAGNER—"PARSIFAL" AND
ITS SIGNIFICANCE

BY

LAWRENCE GILMAN

"So the music of the world flies away from us as we
watch the burning out of the sun. Like bird after bird
its newness flies from us, and finds separate resting-
houses here and there in the places of the past. We who
live and observe whither it has flown have also the privi-
lege of noting the flight of the celestial bird as it leaves
our shores this day for the South that lies behind us."
—VERNON BLACKBURN.

Essay Index Reprint Series

BOOKS FOR LIBRARIES PRESS
FREEPORT, NEW YORK

First Published 1904
Reprinted 1968

TO

PHILIP HALE

WHO IS AMONG THE FOREMOST OF THOSE WHO HAVE
MADE MUSICAL CRITICISM IN AMERICA HONORABLE
AND IMPORTANT, AND WHOSE WORK CANNOT
BUT BE A STIMULUS TO ANY ONE WHO TO-
DAY IS STRIVING TO WRITE SINCERELY,
JUSTLY, AND INDEPENDENTLY UPON
THE SUBTLEST OF THE ARTS

NOTE

OF the twelve papers in this volume, those on MacDowell, Mascagni, and "Parsifal," were published originally in *The North American Review;* the article on Richard Strauss appeared in *The Critic*, and that on "The Question of Realism" in *The Musical Record*. The papers on Elgar, Cornelius, and De Lara's "Messaline" were printed first in *The Musical World*, and the comparative study of Verdi and Wagner and the appreciation of Mr. Loeffler in *The Musician*. The note on Grieg and the essay on "Woman and Modern Music" appeared, respectively, in *Harper's Weekly* and *Harper's*

NOTE

Bazar,—the latter in somewhat different form and under another title.

I take pleasure in acknowledging the courtesy of the editors of these periodicals in permitting me to republish the articles, all of which have been variously altered and amplified.   L. G.

CONTENTS

PHASES OF MODERN MUSIC

THE ACHIEVEMENT OF
RICHARD STRAUSS

"MUSIC had been too long in the laboratories of the wise men. To free it from its Egyptian bondage, to make it the tongue of all life . . ." so aspired Mr. James Huneker's fantastical Piper of Dreams; and so, one likes to imagine, aspired Richard Strauss in the initial moments of his artistic awakening. It is difficult to conceive of a juster verdict upon his essential achievement—if one may venture to appraise it to-day—than that he has accomplished a wider, more searching, more comprehensively inclusive expres-

3

sion of life and experience than music had ever before attempted to compass. He has compelled us to realize that the tone poet fulfils his ultimate purpose only in so far as his art is consistently and richly articulate—only in so far as it is "a tongue of life."

We know what energetic scourgings modern music has received at the hands of no less a personage than Mr. Arnold Dolmetsch. Mr. Dolmetsch, as an incident to a visit which he paid America for the purpose of declaring the virtues of old music, took occasion to instruct a benighted public concerning the deplorable ill which, in his view, had befallen the art in our time. Mr. Dolmetsch saw in the music of modernity a vicious decadence, a perversion of means, a gross and illegitimate expansion. He bewailed the development

4

of musical art away from the naïve
ideals of that elder day of its being
which marked, for him, its apogee,
towards a greater and more complex
significance—the transmutation of an
art that was merely decorative and
accessory into an art that had become
primarily a medium of communication.
And there was profound and sincere
lament for the winsome and quite barren formalities of the days of Scarlatti
and Rameau and Couperin: we were
exhorted to abjure the orchestra and
the piano, and revert to clavichords
and spinets, lutes and virginals and
harpsichords. We were urged to believe that modern music, in attaining
its unique expressional capacity, had
made a reckless and unjustifiable sacrifice of simplicity, reticence, and re-
pose. Mr. Dolmetsch, and those for
whom he is an extravagant mouth-

piece, would have us content ourselves
with mere tonal arabesques — would
convince us that music aims, in the
view of Mr. Daniel Gregory Mason,
"not to represent anything, but to present to the ear and mind combina-
tions of tones which are beautiful in
themselves, and which express no definite ideas." We are tempted to forget that an art—that music—is vital
and valid only in so far as it bears a
direct and verifiable relation to life:
that an art which serves no expressional
need of the human heart or imagination
is an art that can have no abiding
value. For if modern understanding
of its potentialities has taught us anything, it has taught us, with signal impressiveness, that the prime mission of
music is, in the last analysis, precisely
identical with that of those other arts
which have become most finely articu-

late: to be, as the best of critics has
required of poetry, " a criticism of life."
Failing that, it is but the emptiest
of illusive vanities — at most a beautiful embroidery upon life, never its
potent voice and instrument.

Mr. Dolmetsch is right: music has
definitely forsaken prettiness for characterization, an idle loveliness for eloquent signification. But, far as we
have gone, it remained for the great
young master, Richard Strauss, to open
the door into a world—veritable, new,
and of inestimable boundaries—upon
which music had not ventured to im-
pinge. Strauss has, as Mr. Huneker
justly notes, "all the old enchantments
of music; he can woo and ravish the
ear and command the tempests; but
this is not enough. He would have
his art still more definite, his message
still more articulate. . . . Notes, phrases,

groups, movements, masses of tone, no longer occupy the same relative position in his works; they are no longer merely sensuous symbols, but the actual symbols of a language we must hasten to learn, a new speech which relates in wonderful tones wonderful things." He is the most liberating force that music has known since Wagner—the most liberating and the most exhilarating. He touches life at every side—at its most transporting and noblest, at its most quotidian and grotesque: always his aim is to vivify, to quicken, the sense of being. He has written the most humanizing music we possess.

Unlike Wagner, he is concerned, in the main, less with the voicing of elemental emotions through heroic prototypes than with the expression of human experience through the most

8

direct and vivid psychologizing. Such towering figures of beauty and desire as Isolde and Kundry, Siegfried and Wotan, are not of his world. He depends rather upon what one need not hesitate to call a Shakespearian felicity of characterization, of psychological definition. There is nothing in music to parallel the exquisite humanity, the rich and tender comedy, the haunting pathos, of that score in which he is by way of touching hands with the master humanist: I mean his "Don Quixote." Here Strauss is most absolutely, most incontrovertibly, himself; here is the completest measure of his gifts and his capacities.

"Don Quixote" has encountered the usual fate of the contemporary masterwork which is both new in form and of novel content. A score overbrimming with essential humanity and the

9

profoundest comedy, it has been called merely ingenious, a product simply of intellection, a grotesque and derisive parody—nothing more, in fact, than an attempt to excite laughter at the tribulations of the illuded knight. And yet it is increasingly difficult to understand how it is possible to lend one's self unreservedly to the direct appeal of this fascinating and most moving score, and fail to perceive the ripe emotion, the infinitely compassionate humor, which inspired it. Mr. Ernest Newman, one of the few acute and untrammelled admirers of the Munich tone-poet, properly and discerningly insists upon the " perfect humanity " of " Don Quixote "; he notes how tender the characterization is throughout, how exquisitely human is the feeling for " these two poor tragi-comic actors." It is that which finally makes the

work so precious—"its unfailing pity,
its intuitive avoidance of anything that
would make it simply unthinking
comedy." That is justly and aptly said.
I, for one, am aware of no more felici-
tous, more poignant characterization in
music than that of the absurdly valorous, dream-haunted knight, with his
preposterous ambitions, his native sweetness, his impulsive and touching ardors;
nor of any page more pitiful, more
emotive, than the latter portion of the
tenth variation, depicting the grievous
home-coming of the broken-hearted Don
after his defeat by the Knight of the
White Moon; nor of any music in which
is to be found a nobler utterance of
rapturous contemplation than is to be
found in the third variation, wherein
the Knight discourses fervently upon
the rewards and glories of romantic
chivalry; and how insistent is the

pathos, the grave simplicity, of the
death scene! It is a very great, a
very lovable work, this opus 35 of
Strauss. "Die Meistersinger" is its
only musical analogue; but even that
delectable masterpiece, for all its superlative loveliness, its engrossing gayety
and sentiment, falls short of the younger
work in depth and import. In "Don
Quixote" is that "laughter of reason
refreshed," which, as Mr. Meredith tells
us, "is floriferous, like the magical
great gale of the shifty spring decid-
ing for summer"; here, too, is that
laughter of the spirit which perceives
the incongruous because it divines at
the same time an ultimate harmony
and perfectness, an ultimate fulfilment.

I have ventured to call "Don
Quixote" Strauss's most generic and
representative achievement. His "Zarathustra," magnificently audacious,

magnificently original as it is, is, on
the whole, a less consummate accomplishment; there are suggestions of rhetoric, of inflated portentousness, which
do not declare the better Strauss; and
the theatric posing of the "great earth-
riddle" at the close is unconvinc-
ing. Nor does the "Heldenleben,"
superbly powerful and effective as
it is, quite justify its flamboyant he-
roics. With Mr. Newman, I should be
astonished, and sorry, to hear that
Strauss set very much store by the
significance of this score. Is it not
likely, as Mr. Newman suggests, that
Strauss, "after a good many years of
intense cerebration and of multitudinous
experiences of the stupidity of the
human race towards a new musician,
had resolved to have a little semi-
playful fling for his own satisfaction,
the result being 'Ein Heldenleben'"? It

is scarcely possible to believe that Strauss intended seriously the self-glorification implied by the deliberate quotation of passages from his earlier works, adduced for the confusion of his imagined critics. His latest production, also, the "Symphonia Domestica," one is compelled to appraise as a jest of Brobdingnagian proportions, despite much that it has of persuasiveness and sincere emotion. Even the warmest adherent of the Straussian gospel must prefer to regard other than gravely the attempt to give indiscriminate musical utterance to the manifold activities of the family circle. Concerning "Till Eulenspiegel" there is little to say save in praise of its amazing virtuosity and its Rabelaisian humors; this is frankly a diversion, an exuberant burlesque.

Of the earlier tone-poems, "Don Juan," "Macbeth," and "Tod und

Verklärung"—the first three of the
epoch-making list—it has become traditional to take but brief and cursory
note. One finds, it is true, comparatively
little of the present Strauss in them, and
a considerable infusion of Liszt and
Wagner. But in one of them, at least—
"Tod und Verklärung"—Strauss has
written with a burning beauty, an
ecstatic conviction, a gravity of impli-
cation which, despite an occasional
derivation from one or the other of his
most influential masters, are not surpassed in anything that he has since
done. If "Don Quixote" is his most
richly human and most musically representative work, "Tod und Verklärung" is most profound in its significance
of content. Composed in 1897, it is only
the third of the eight orchestral masterpieces upon which his great fame chiefly
rests; and yet it is doubtful if he will

ever give us anything so important in idea and substance—if he will ever utter, with so unexampled a conviction and impressiveness, aspirations and imaginings of such overpowering moment. In this score, at least, he has touched the margin of the sublime.

The idea of death, and that consternation and despair and anguish which are its human ministers, could have no more complete and wonderful an expression than they have here. Strauss, in his terrible and splendid celebration of the supreme event, has completed that message in whose deliverance the voice of Tschaikowsky, in that other canticle of mortality, the "Pathetic Symphony," faltered and broke; and in the profound and entire contrast of these two great works is, if one chooses to discern it, the pointing of a spiritual moral. One could not better indicate the nature of Strauss's accomplishment in "Tod und Verklärung" than by setting it, for a moment, beside the work of the Slavonic master.

Mr. Vernon Blackburn has compared Tschaikowsky's beautiful threnody with Shelley's "Adonais," which, he says, is its counterpart in literature; for as "'time,' writes Shelley, 'like a many-colored dome of glass, stains the white radiance of eternity,' even so Tschaikowsky in this symphony has stained eternity's radiance; he has captured the years and bound them into a momentary emotional pang." And Mr. Blackburn speaks with felicity and emotion of "this wonderful and extraordinary work, . . . which shakes the heart and fills up all one's lifelong grief for things that are dead." A wonderful and extraordinary work indeed! What Shelley,

17

no doubt, would have said in the utterance of his great grief, had Shelley been a musician, Tschaikowsky says in his most affecting swan - song. Here is music, declares Mr. Blackburn, passionately avid of life for life's own sake— music filled, from beginning to end, "with the utter and complete darkness of the grave."

I have alleged Mr. Blackburn's analysis of the essential mood of the " Pathétique " because he exposes so aptly the significance of its impulse and its appeal. The finality of death — the irrevocable oblivion of the grave—an inappeasable and hopeless grieving: that, indisputably, is the emotional substance of Tschaikowsky's tone-poem; that, beyond question, is what it says, and all that it says. One hears in it the despairful cry of that bravest optimist of them all, in one of those "downcast

18

hours" which at times afflicted even his most valorous and steadfast spirit:

"Matter is conqueror — matter, triumphant only, continues onward."

Tschaikowsky reveals himself in this, his undoubted masterpiece, as the perfect materialist, the perfect spiritual craven. That stupendous *adagio lamentoso* is a sable "garment of untruth," dyed with the hues that are gathered out of cowardice, and despair, and ignoble and supine grief. His was a mind "held ever earthward on the trail of earthly things"; his was the point of view, the spiritual outlook, of the essential barbarian—"the barbarian," as Mr. Blackburn himself has somewhere said, "smitten by the musical *Zeitgeist*." That is true of the musician, and it is true of the man. Taking him humanly, rather than musically—the soul in him rather than the artist in him: a barbarian smitten by the *Zeitgeist* — that, to my seeing, is the Tschaikowsky of the "Pathétique." He has given, in this most intimate of his disclosures, a superlatively beautiful and puissant expression to that in himself, and in us, which is most unreclaimably and grossly earthbound—to the animal, to the vestige of the savage in us: to that lamentation over the precious things of the sensual life which, communicating its panic and despair to all who hear, diverts the eyes from the vision of those immutable things by virtue of whose perception alone do we approach the gods. For those of us to whom this world seems not wholly illdesigned, who find no shuddering horror in the thought of death, but rather a surety of promotion and fulfilment— for those of us, I say, who so incline, this music overwhelms with the sense of an immense and futile pathos, and a tragic falsity as maleficent as it is complete.

Turn, now, to a consideration, from the spiritual side, of Strauss's magnificent elegy, whose greatness a comparison with Tschaikowsky's symphony throws into a heightened light.

Here is a stupendously eloquent enunciation of the terror, the awe, the pathos, of the essential episode of death, but, also, of the majesty and perfection of a triumphant spiritual survival. I am fully aware that this is praise of a work which has been disposed of by some as "charnel-house" music, the unwholesome issue of a disordered imagination—what excess of morbidly realistic imagery has not been discovered in Strauss's score by certain critical intelligences? And yet I prefer rather to agree with the view of Mr.

Philip Hale, that here is music "in which there is no morbid taint, in which there is the full justification of death." And how wonderful a justification! What a solemn and haunting tenderness, what a continuity of sheer loveliness, in the brooding passages of the opening—and how keenly the dominant mood, the atmosphere of the thing, engages one from the start; what an immensity of passion in the phases of revolt and aspiration, and how appalling is the moment of translation! But—and here is the significant point—Strauss does not stop at that portentous episode, that heart-chilling crisis of extreme dismay; death is not for him, as for Tschaikowsky, an inexorable conclusion, an irretrievable exit: he confronts us, as we are confronted in the "Pathétique," with the very gates of death, but, unlike Tschaikowsky, he does not leave us

22

there, overwhelmed and shuddering in the darkness. Out of that terrible quietude emerges an increasing chant, a gradual and suffusing radiance. Note by note the transfiguration is accomplished—"and when he is wrapt by the radiance, the bright one no longer sees dreams; then within him the bliss arises": so may one point the moral of a tone-poem of to-day with the immemorial wisdom of the East!

If I can find so luminous and high a message in "Tod und Verklärung," I shall scarcely assume to regard Richard Strauss as a deliberate and conscious seer; and I doubt if he would care, or if he deserves, to be called a mystic. Great musician and poet that he is, he is neither so deep nor so wide as the "Upanishads." But I shall insist, nevertheless, upon claiming for him that he has, after some manner of his own, "beheld the indwelling spirit"; and that in this work he has chosen, "knowing that knowable spirit," to say to us, with the incomparable prophet of the Orient: "Let not death disturb you."

It is scarcely necessary to attempt, in this place, to contravene the familiar accusations of wanton ugliness, of perverseness and morbidity of motive, which mar so many contemporary estimates of Strauss. Nor need one re-echo facile praise of those inescapable and merely contributive excellences which have served as the obscuring trees in the wood for those who are blind to the fundamental greatness of the man: enough—proportionately too much, indeed—has been said of his astounding technical mastership, the unequalled complexity of the apparatus which he chooses to employ. Instead, let it be

RICHARD STRAUSS

affirmed simply that Richard Strauss is an artist of profound and just convictions, the most penetrant and sympathetic of humanists—that here, finally, at the beginning of a new century, is one who serves as a transcendent exemplification of the essential musician of modernity. He speaks a language whose unique capacity it is to embody all intense and valid phases of experience: that reflects an art which is, with memorable consistency, "steeped in the colors of human life."

AN AMERICAN TONE-POET

WHEN Mr. Ernest Newman, an English critic of acuity, remarked in a recent essay that the Romantic movement in music had "done its work,"—though "even in our own day it still makes an occasional ineffectual effort to raise its old head, ludicrous now with its faded garlands of flowers,"—it must doubtless have seemed to many that he spoke with point and justification. Indisputably the Romanticism which Mr. Newman meant — the Romanticism which expended itself in the fabrication of a pasteboard world of "gloomy forests, enchanted castles, impossible maidens, and the obsolete profession of magic"—

26

has had its day, and now seems, in the retrospect, incredibly puerile, incredibly fatuous and wrong. But this was the Romanticism of perverted sentiment—a false thing, a mistaken thing, a thing of "vain shows and shadows and ideals." There is another Romance: a spirit incomparably fresh and vital, a primeval impulse and aspiration, that is not barren and moribund, but quick and increasing. "Through the heart," says Fiona Macleod in one of her most haunting pages, "through the heart I go to lost gardens, to mossed fountains, to groves where is no white beauty of still statue, but only the beauty of an old forgotten day." There, by those fountains, and in those groves and gardens, flowers that immemorial Romance of the transforming imagination. It is a Romance that is in no wise divorced from reality—that is, in fact,

27

but reality imaginatively apprehended;
if it uses the old Romanticistic properties, it uses them, not as substantives,
but as symbols of intense emotional
realities. For the essential romanticist
and the essential realist are fundamentally at one — save for differences that
are merely temperamental — in their
primary purpose to represent "the
thing as in itself it really is"; and it is
in no sort an accusation against realism
if one attempts to define those differences by saying that, in its finest
estate, the romantic spirit concerns
itself with essences rather than with
details, with impressions rather than
with documents, with the heightened
expression of spiritual substance rather
than with literal representation. Which
is merely to say that it deals in a truth
that is no less truth because it is reflected
imaginatively, and through a beauty

28

that may often be in the last degree incalculable and aërial.

It is this authentic spirit of romance
that has an exquisite life in certain music
of to-day—pre-eminently, I think, in the
work of an American composer: Edward
MacDowell. I account Mr. MacDowell
so notably a romantic of the finer order
because, true to the subtler genius of his
art, he devotes himself, in his practice
of it, to a rendering—extraordinary for
vividness and felicity—of those essences
and impressions which have seemed to
me to be the ultimate concern of the
romantic spirit in its dealings with life.
He has chosen occasionally to employ,
in the realization of his purposes, what
seems at first to be precisely the magical
apparatus so necessary to the older
Romanticism—dryads and elves inhabit
his world, and he dwells at times under
faery boughs and in enchanted woods;

but for him, as for the poets of the Celtic tradition, these things are but the manifest images of an interior passion and delight. Seen in the transfiguring mirror of his music, the moods and events of the natural world and of the incessant drama of psychic life are vivified into shapes and designs of ineluctable beauty and appeal.

Both in theory and in practice, Mr. MacDowell stands uncompromisingly for music that is, of intention, persistently pictorial and impressionistic. Thus his themes are Lancelot and Elaine, Arthur, The Gaelic Cuchullin, the sea, a deserted farm, a water-lily, meadow brooks and will-o'-the-wisps, starlight, a haunted house, a wild rose— a poet, it will be observed, enamoured of "the mystery and the majesty of earth," although scarcely less thrall to purely human emotion. If one is, at

times, inclined to praise in him the poet
of the natural world at the expense of
the musical humanist, it is because he
is, constitutionally and by right of
ancestry, Celtic of the Celts, with the
Celt's intimate vision of natural things,
and his magic power of poetically vivifying them. Again and again is it borne
in upon one, in considering his work,
that this tone-poet of the natural world
is striking that "sheer, inimitable,
Celtic note" which we have been
taught so readily to recognize in another art, and striking it with an astonishing surety, an inextinguishable
ardor and inspiration. It is making
no transcendent claim for him to affirm
that in such splendid fantasies as his
"To the Sea," "In Mid-Ocean," "In
Deep Woods"; in such sensitive impressions as "Starlight," "To a Water-
Lily," "To a Wild Rose," there is an

31

inevitable felicity, a graphic nearness
and beauty, an imaginative intensity
and lyric fervor which exist nowhere
in external tone-painting save in Mr.
MacDowell's own work.

Music, of course—from Haydn to
Wagner and Raff—abounds in examples
of eloquent natural imagery. One need
not, in claiming a certain excellence
for him, imply that Mr. MacDowell has ever threatened the suprem-
acy of such things as the "Rheingold" *Vorspiel* or the "Walküre" fire
music. It is as much in his choice
of subjects as in the peculiar felicity
of his expression that he is unique
among tone-poets of the external world.
He has never attempted such tremendous frescoes as Wagner delighted to
paint; nor does he choose to deal with
the elements—with winds and waters,
with fire and clouds and tempests—

32

in the epical manner of the great music-dramatist. Of his descriptive music by far the greater part is written for the piano, so that, at the start, a very definite limitation is imposed upon magnitude of plan. You cannot achieve on the piano, with any adequacy of effect, a mountain-side in flames, or a storm at sea, or the prismatic arch of a rainbow; and as Mr. MacDowell has seen fit to employ that instrument as his principal medium of expression, he has refrained from attempting to advance musical fresco-painting beyond the point at which Wagner left it. Instead, he has contented himself with such themes as he treats in his "Forest Idyls," in his "Four Little Poems" ("The Eagle," "The Brook," "Moonshine," "Winter"), in his first orchestral suite, in the inimitable "Woodland Sketches" and "Sea Pieces," and in the recently pub-

lished "New England Idyls." As a
perfect exemplification of his practice,
consider—let me say—his "To a Water-
Lily," from the "Woodland Sketches "—
than which I know of nothing in objective
tone-painting, for the piano or for the
orchestra, more justly felt, more exquisitely accomplished. The method is
the method of Shelley in the "Sensitive
Plant," of Wordsworth in "The Daffodils," as it is the method of Raff
rather than of Wagner—although Raff
could never have written with precisely
that order of delicate eloquence. The
thing is steeped in loveliness, in sheer
natural magic. So in his "Wild Rose,"
in his "Starlight," in his " Wandering
Iceberg," in his "To the Sea": always
he is the admirable poet, intent upon
realizing, through the medium of tones
rather than of words, a deep and intimate vision of the natural world. And

he can persuade you, too, with *Forgael*, of "the streams where the world ends"—

"Where time is drowned in odor-laden winds
And druid moons, and murmuring of
  boughs. . . ."

What an aërial and gleaming magic in his "Nautilus"!—that misty and spell-bound vision wherein

". . . a ship of pearl
  Under a silken sail and a silver yard"

drifts upon shining waters under "glimmering winds" — music in which the mood is so tenuous, the emotion so incalculable and evanescent, that it seems scarcely to have a credible existence as material fact.

It would be unjust, though it would not be inexcusable, to give too great a prominence, in considering Mr. Mac-Dowell's work, to his poetry of nature.

35

For if he has a rapt delight in the moods of winds and waves and the elemental life of the forest, he is even more deeply engrossed in the contemplation of those ways and workings of the primeval human heart which are, after all, the ultimate concern of music. If, in his own field, he is inimitable as the poet of the "Sea Pieces," he measures up to the height of eminent names as the author of the "Four Songs" (opus 56), "A Deserted Farm," "Told at Sunset," the "Scotch Poem," the four sonatas, and certain of the "New England Idyls." Here, certainly, are profound emotion, a deep and transporting tenderness—an "eloquence of the heart"—in which again one is tempted to trace the essential Celt.

I do not know if a remoter verdict will award Mr. MacDowell greater honor as a writer for the voice or for instruments—certainly it is rash to be over-positive in decision upon the relative value of such work as, on the one hand, "The Four Songs," and, on the other, the "Keltic" Sonata; but, for my own part, I must believe that, admirably affecting song-writer as he is, Mr. MacDowell has never equalled, certainly never surpassed, that work of his which I have already named—the "Keltic" Sonata, his fourth in E minor. With the publication of this work, his opus 59, Mr. MacDowell achieved a conclusive and emphatic demonstration of his capacity as a creative artist of indubitable consequence. Not before had he given us so convincing an earnest of the larger aspect of his genius—neither in the three earlier sonatas nor in the *Indian Suite* has he attained an equal magnitude, an equal scope and significance. This is unquestionably, so far,

his masterpiece. Mr. MacDowell's genius has here found its consummate flow-
ering. Nowhere else in his work are
its distinguishing traits so strikingly
disclosed — the breadth and reach of
imagination, the magnetic vitality, the
richness and fervor, the conquering
poetic charm. Here you will find "the
beauty of wildness," and "the beauty
of sorrowful things"; "the beauty of the
men that take up spears and die for a
name"; "the beauty of the poets that
take up harp and sorrow and the wandering road"—a harp shaken with a wild
and piercing music, a sorrow that is not
of to-day, but of a past when dreams
were actual and imperishable, and men
lived the tales of beauty and of wonder which now are but a discredited and
fading memory.

It was a fortunate, if not an inevitable, event, in view of his temperamental

38

affiliations with the Celtic genius, that
Mr. MacDowell should have been made
aware of the suitability for musical
treatment of the ancient heroic chron-
icles of the Gaels, and that he should
have gone for his inspiration, in particular, to the legends comprised in the
famous Cycle of the Red Branch. In
a motto with which he prefixes the
sonata he gives this index to its poetic
content:

> "Who minds now Keltic tales of yore,
> Dark druid rhymes that thrall,
> Deirdré's song and wizard lore
> Of great Cuchullin's fall."

Mr. MacDowell has attempted no mere
musical recounting of those romances
of the ancient Gaelic world at which he
hints in these lines. He has aimed to
make his music, he says, "more a commentary on the subject than an actual

4

depiction of it"; but to say that he has realized vividly and beautifully all that this denotes—all that which is essentially implicit in the source of his inspiration—would be but a niggardly statement of the truth. It would be juster to say, rather, that he has recalled in his music the very life and presence of the Gaelic prime—that he has indeed "unbound the Island harp." Above all, he has achieved that "heroic beauty" which, believes Mr. Yeats, has been fading out of the arts since "that decadence we call progress set voluptuous beauty in its place"—that heroic beauty which is of the very essence of the imaginative life of the primitive Celts, and which the Celtic "revival" in contemporary letters has so singularly failed to recrudesce. For it is the heroic Gaelic world that Mr. MacDowell has made to live again in his music—that miraculous

40

world of superhuman passions and aspirations, of bards and heroes and sublime adventure—the world of Cuchullin the Unconquerable, and Laeg, and Queen Meave; of Naesi, and Deirdré the Beautiful, and Fergus, and Connla the Harper, and those kindred figures, lovely or greatly tragical, that are like no other figures in the world's mythologies.

That this is music which challenges the imagination is undeniable. It makes small appeal to the tonal sense *per se*— to the sense which craves in music merely, in Wagner's phrase, "the susciting of pleasure in beautiful forms." Mr. MacDowell does not write what we presume to call "absolute" music; if one looks to such a work as the "Keltic" Sonata for the kind of gratification which he is accustomed to derive from, for example, a Brahms symphony, he will not find it. It is impossible to account satisfactorily for the last page of the "Keltic" upon exclusively musical grounds; it is as essentially—though not so avowedly — programmatic as the "Scotch Poem" of opus 31, and, as with that swift and graphic paraphrase, its ultimate appeal is conditioned upon an understanding of the basis of drama and emotional crisis upon which the musician has built. Ernest Newman has effectually exposed the absurdity of the popular sophistry which concedes the legitimacy of programme music so long as it sounds "as well as absolute music to any one who does not know the story"; so I need not concern myself with a quite superfluous apology for Mr. MacDowell's indifference to the dicta of the absolutists. But while I must admit his usual indifference, I cannot help wishing that he might contrive some expedient for doing away, so far as he himself is

concerned, with the sonata form which
he occasionally uses, rather incon-
sistently, as a vehicle for the expression
of that vision and emotion that are in
him; for, generally speaking, and in
spite of the triumphant success of the
"Keltic," Mr. MacDowell is less fortunate in his sonatas than in those
freer and more elastically wrought
tone-poems in which he voices a mood
or an experience with epigrammatic
concision and directness. The "Keltic" succeeds in spite of its form —
as the earlier "Norse," "Eroica," and
"Tragica" sonatas do not, at all points
—through sheer force of inspiration;
though even here, and notwithstanding
the freedom of manipulation, one feels
that he would have worked to still
finer ends in a more flexible and fluent
form. He is never so compelling, so
persuasively eloquent, as in those im-

pressionistically conceived pieces in
which he moulds his inspiration upon
the events of an interior emotional
programme, rather than upon a musical
formula necessarily arbitrary and anom-
alous — in such things, for instance, as
the "Idyls" and "Poems" after Goethe
and Heine, the "Woodland Sketches,"
the "Sea Pieces," the "Fireside Tales,"
the "New England Idyls," the Raff-
like orchestral suite, opus 42, and
the symphonic poems "Hamlet and
Ophelia," "Lancelot and Elaine," and
"The Saracens" and "Lovely Alda"
(both after the Song of Roland). Here
he is invulnerably himself.

Of MacDowell the technician, the musical artist, one is tempted to dispose
by saying that he is of the prophets
of modernity; but he is more, and he
is somewhat less, than that too-facile
phrase would connote: a master of

44

harmonic effort, he is yet persistently and frankly melodic—melodic with a suppleness, a breadth, a directness and spontaneity which one knows in Franz and in Schubert, but which one scarcely looks for in a contemporary of Debussy and Younger Russia. He knows the secret of a melody which can be at once spontaneous and subtle, at once fluent and distinguished. His insistence upon the value and importance of the *melos* is, probably, his most striking characteristic; and it is in this that he is, one may say, both behind and in advance of his time.

Mr. MacDowell is to-day an artistic figure of commanding stature—a musical creator who has brought to an impressive development a singular gift of beautiful and forceful utterance. He is a poet among musicians, and an authentic genius.

45

CONCERNING EDWARD ELGAR

SIR EDWARD ELGAR, the English composer, has been uncommonly fortunate in his critics. Mr. Vernon Blackburn, one of the most eminent of the craft in Great Britain, has declared him an equal, in certain respects, of Beethoven; and no creative achievement in recent music has evoked such instant and extraordinary laudation as has been, from the very first, the portion of Elgar's most successful work, "The Dream of Gerontius." When Mr. Blackburn, writing immediately after its production at the Birmingham festival of 1900, virtually declared it to be the finest musical work since Wagner, he

pitched the key for the pæan of ac-
clamation which has everywhere greeted
the cantata upon its subsequent performances. It has not been thought
extravagant to discover in it the logical
successor of "Parsifal," and the most
admirable accomplishment in English
music since Purcell. Richard Strauss
was pleased to praise it, and Richter in-
scribed a quaint and fervid encomium
in the orchestral score after his con-
ducting of the original performance.
With such a reputation, it was no more
than natural that Elgar's work should
have aroused in this country the most
eager and expectant interest. Of the
immediate and positive success which
signalized its American production one
need not speak; the fact has passed
into familiar history. But has Elgar's
music the great and important excellence that is claimed for it? It will

47

not be unjust to regard "The Dream of Gerontius" and his later work, "The Apostles," as representative achievements, and to consider them as such.

It must be said, at the start, that "The Dream of Gerontius" is as far as possible from being a replica of the traditional oratorio form which has so long shackled the minds and the imaginations of English composers. Nothing could be less Mendelssohnian, less English in a particular sense, than this masterpiece of the most eminent of living English musicians. It marks as sharp a departure from the jejune and outworn formulæ of the typical British builder of oratorios as the early utterances of Wagner's genius did from the prevailing traditions of the operatic stage of that day. Elgar has not hesitated to cast his work uncompromisingly in the mould of the modern lyric drama. He has dispensed with the cumbrous and pedantic formalities so precious in the sight of his predecessors —the exigently academic soul will find nothing in Elgar's score to satisfy its demand for set numbers, although it will find a sufficiency of very dexterous contrapuntal writing. The music flows without break or artificial pause, reflecting throughout the dramatic and emotional content of the text. Admirably fluent, various, and responsive, the orchestra, the chorus, and the solo voices serve as a unified and elastic vehicle for the embodiment of the profoundly moving and noble poem which Elgar has chosen for his subject.

As in its construction, so in its spirit and conception is this score a new and revealing thing in English music. An incorrigible mystic, Cardinal Newman's intensely religious fantasy of the

49

perilous translation of a human soul
from its mortal case into the veiled and
awful presence of its God has inspired
him to a musical expression conceived
upon a plane of the most exalted and
sustained nobility. Nothing more deeply sincere, more ardent in its aspiration,
more rapt and incessant in its exaltation, has come out of modern music
since Wagner imagined his majestic
Parable of the Grail. For the devout
and beautiful spirit in which Elgar's
music is steeped from beginning to end
there can be nothing but the most
unqualified praise; but with this, one
reaches the bounds of a justifiable
admiration. Elgar has been unable
to transmute his wholly genuine piety
and fervor into music of authentic and
individual inspiration. When one re-
calls Vernon Blackburn's vision of him
"waiting for ten years without putting

pen to paper until the dew of inspiration had fallen upon his spirit," one can only bow one's head in humble silence and meditate upon the disheartening futility of the critical function; for that seems to me precisely to connote what Elgar has not done. If any dew of inspiration fell upon his spirit during the composition of "The Dream of Gerontius," it has singularly failed to precipitate itself in the music.

It would be absurd to deny that there are many moments of intense and beautiful expression in the work—moments in which Elgar has realized the precise emotion of the text with most extreme and affecting eloquence. But the eloquence is not "self-sprung": it is not Elgar's; it is Wagner's. He speaks often with the tongues of men and of angels, but they are the men and the angels of Wagner; they are Tristan, and Parsifal, and Amfortas, and the transfigured chorus of the Monsalvat sanctuary. There would be little profit, I conceive, in exploring Elgar's score for specific examples of his dependence upon Wagner; nor would such a proceeding subserve the finer ends of justice; for Elgar has so saturated himself with Wagner's idiom, his manner of musical speech, that passages which seem at first almost like intentional transcriptions are no doubt quite unconsciously and quite innocently reproduced. It is not so much because certain of his phrases seem modelled, note for note, upon Wagnerian patterns that one must insist upon the magnitude of his debt to that fatally compelling master; it is rather because Elgar himself has no distinction of speech, no personal habit of expression, to counterbalance any pardonable derivation from Wagner which he might occasionally permit himself (consider the degree in which even that most implacably individual of modern music-makers, Richard Strauss, resorts to a purely Wagnerian utterance in his " Tod und Verklärung " and " Zarathustra "). He has not yet, as Mr. John F. Runciman observed some years ago, evolved an individual style. One cannot put one's finger upon any single passage in his score and say, "This, beyond dispute, is Elgar: here is a quality of beauty, of emotion, of personality, which is absolutely native and unique." Those portions of " The Dream of Gerontius " which one can unhesitatingly assert to be his own are, in the main, without potency, without distinction, without significance. As Mr. Runciman has acutely remarked, "he is obsessed a little by the common academic idea that anything is good enough for the theme, and that the beginning and the end of music consist in ingenuity of treatment." One must concede at once that Elgar has achieved some admirable pages—that he has written, at times, with undeniable loveliness, with undeniable power and effect. How beautiful, for example, is that passage in E-flat major which accompanies the words of the Angel of the Agony when he pleads with Jesu to "spare these souls which are so dear to Thee"! Nor could anything be more richly impressive than the superb D major section for chorus, orchestra, and the voice of the ministering priest, wherein the passing soul of Gerontius is exhorted to go forth "in the name of God"; and the climax wherewith Elgar contrives to suggest, in a passage of overwhelming eloquence, the stupendous

54

disclosure of the majesty of God, is nothing short of magnificent.

But how banal, on the other hand, is the opening recitative of Gerontius—"Jesu, Maria, I am near to death, and Thou art calling me"! how unresourceful the treatment of such passages as "Rouse thee, my fainting soul, and play the man"! And how conventional is the credo: "Firmly I believe and truly God is Three and God is One"! I shall not go so far as to say, with Mr. Henry T. Finck, that Elgar has written merely *Kapellmeistermusik;* and yet, when one notes the complacently perfunctory character of many of his themes, one comes to feel that the epithet may not be, after all, unnecessarily harsh. His choral writing is, of course, masterly, from the standpoint of sheer technical brilliancy; and he rises at times—in, for instance, the demon scene and the

5   55

"Praise to the Holiest" chorus — to points of extreme effectiveness; but here again, as in his writing for the solo voices, the melodic texture is not of first-rate inspiration.

His scoring is modern and vivid, at all times adequate, plastic, and picturesque; but as for Elgar's going far beyond Wagner in his treatment of the orchestra (to adopt the phrase of one of his more vivacious admirers)—that, I should say, verges dangerously upon the hyperbolic.

To conclude: I cannot believe that in "The Dream of Gerontius" Elgar has produced a work of more than respectable attainments; nor am I at all sure that its primacy in modern English music has, after all, been established so very clearly and indubitably. Is not the work of G. W. L. Marshall-Hall—whom Mr. Runciman sets in the front rank of contemporary British composers

—of very considerable importance? Has not Fritz Delius written music at least equal in beauty and modernity to what we know of the work of Elgar? And are the achievements of Coleridge-Taylor entirely negligible? The question is, I think, altogether indeterminate and debatable.

Concerning Elgar's later and equally famous work, "The Apostles," critical opinion in England has been less unified. The work had its initial performance in October, 1903, at the Birmingham festival, and raised almost as much expository dust as its more admired predecessor. To some, "The Apostles" revealed itself as "a masterpiece, an invaluable contribution to the art of the world, a score of pure gold throughout"—thus the impulsive Mr. Blackburn. To Mr. Ernest Newman, on the other hand—and Mr. Newman, let it be noted, is a friend and sincere admirer of Elgar—the music seemed "not sufficiently inspired to satisfy the musical mind," and "impressive only to minds that are already disposed to consider anything beautiful that is associated with a sacred text."—There, probably, is the crux of the matter.

Elgar planned, in his own words, "to compose an oratorio which should embody the calling of the Apostles, their teaching (schooling), and their mission in the establishment of the Church among the Gentiles." The first two parts of the work have for their theme the outward manifestation of God to those "who were called," completed in the ascension; the third and final section, as yet* unfinished, will deal with the inward manifestation of God

* August, 1904.

"through His indwelling Spirit." The
basis of the work is thus, it will be
seen, essentially theological, and Elgar,
himself devoutly ecclesiastical in his
point of approach, has furnished forth
his text with music of fervid sincerity
and conviction. Let it be said without
qualification that the score of "The
Apostles," considered solely as a structural achievement, is superbly successful;
its complexity of texture, its subtlety of
elaboration—in brief, its sheer mastery
of musical mechanics—are nothing short
of amazing; but there, in my view,
praise must stop. As in the case of "The
Dream of Gerontius," one's deliberate
criticism of this score is that it has nothing unique, nothing new, to say. It
has little of the impressive, though un-
individualized, beauty of its predecessor. Its best inspirations are, in essence,
a dilution of Wagner; that which is

not best is Elgar's own, and is, in the main, dull, unleavened, inexpressive. There are, indeed, a few exceptions—as the introduction, the dawn music, the final chorus—the merits of which one concedes at once. One must end, though, by echoing Mr. Newman in his dislike of "The Apostles," "with"—as he complains—"its heavy atmosphere, its monotonous rhythms, its dragging, enervated pulses."

It would be pleasant further to coincide with Mr. Newman in his confident belief in the preciousness of Elgar's gifts, which, he believes, must have come to a finer fulfilment had they not been "taken from humanity in order to be given to the Church"; but here, unfortunately, one must dissent.

CHARLES MARTIN LOEFFLER

MR. CHARLES MARTIN LOEFFLER, an
Alsatian by birth but a Bostonian by
profession, occupies a peculiar place,
entirely of his own creation, in the field
of contemporary music. He is a seeker
after the realities of shadowy and dim
illusions, an artist in grays and greens
and subtle golds. The opulent purples
in which Richard Strauss delights, with
the exuberance of his fiery temperament, have no attraction for Mr.
Loeffler. The insistent appeal, the expected richness, the continual irides-
cence of Strauss's schemes are quite
absent from the strange and intimate
music of this tonal Verlaine. Mr. Loef-

fler is of "the children of revery," a
weaver of dreams. For him, indeed,
shadows and dreams are the invincible
realities, and from them he derives a
compelling music—music which serenely
rebukes dissection.

That serenity, that innocence of intention, are, indeed, remarkable. After
the plangent splendors, the torrential
rhetoric, of the amazing Strauss, the
music of Mr. Loeffler, owning something
of the subdued and elusive beauty of
antique tapestries, addresses the spirit
with a unique appeal. Where Strauss
is challenging, importunate, Mr. Loeffler persuades—not with the personal
concern of the advocate, for his detachment, and, as I have said, his
innocence of intention, are as entire
as they are sincere — but, as it were,
in spite of himself. "There," you hear
him saying (if you can imagine him

sufficiently self-conscious), "is the result of an absorbing experience: I have been reading that perturbing drama of Maurice Maeterlinck's, 'La Mort de Tintagiles,' and have tried to put into music my impressions of it, perhaps finding a definiteness of emotion in its essential substance which Maeterlinck has not denoted; it may possibly interest you." And he leaves it for you to receive it as you like.

His is music in which the emotion conveyed is the emotion of remembered rapture, the beauty, "the surviving beauty óf gathered dreams" — seldom the emotion and the beauty of that which is actual and present. Mr. Loeffler is most urgently aroused by such moods of longing and remote enchantment as find jeweled expression in the "Timbres Oubliés" of Gustave Kahn, for which he has written unforgettable music:

63

"Timbres oubliés des charmants jardins,
Timbres argentins des Thulés lointains,
Timbres violets des voix consolantes
Épandant graves les bénédictions,
Timbres bleus des péris aux féeries,
Timbres d'or des mongoles orfèvreries
Et vieil or des vieilles nations!"

Nor does his habit of artistic speech tempt him to such outbursts of passionate lament as fill the utterances, say, of Tschaikowsky's genius with so insupportable a poignancy. Mr. Loeffler perceives his world with as rapt a gaze, with as complete an absorption in its emotional panorama, as the most vivid and declamatory of the moderns; but the issue of his understanding is a certain veiled and continent intensity, an interior passion, a conviction implied rather than declared. That is, finally, the peculiarity of his art.

Of Loeffler the man, viewing him biographically, let it suffice to say that he was born in Mülhausen, Upper Alsace, forty-three years ago; that he received the greater part of his musical training in France, Belgium, and Germany; that he came to America twenty-four years ago, and now, as he confesses, "feels somewhat of a foreigner" when he visits Germany or France. He was for some years the second concertmaster of the Boston Symphony Orchestra, sharing the desk occupied at the time by Franz Kneisel—for he is an admirable virtuoso as well as a composer of rare endowments.

Of his listed works—published or in manuscript—there are, for orchestra: "Les Veillées de l'Ukraine," a suite in four movements based upon tales by Gogol; the symphonic poem, "La Mort de Tintagiles," after the marionette drama by Maeterlinck; and "Two Poems" —the first after the lovely aubade from Verlaine's "La Bonne Chanson,"

"Avant que tu ne t'en ailles," the second after Rollinat's "Villanelle du Diable." There is also a Divertimento for violin and orchestra; a cello concerto; an octet for two clarinets, two violins, viola, cello, double-bass, and harp; a sextet for strings; a quintet for three violins, viola, and cello; two rhapsodies for oboe, viola, and piano, after poems by Rollinat; a "Poëme Païen" for two pianos and three trumpets (the latter behind the scenes). And there are songs with words by Verlaine, Baudelaire, Gustave Kahn—some with viola obligato.

A cosmopolitan, a man of ripe and sensitive culture, Mr. Loeffler finds his richest inspiration in that literature which the inconsiderate have disposed of, to their apparent satisfaction, as "decadent"—as in his symphonic poem, "La Mort de Tintagiles," based on the drama of Maeterlinck, in the "Two Poems" for orchestra inspired by the verse of Verlaine and Rollinat, and in his recent "Quatre Mélodies pour chant et piano," which are settings of poems by Gustave Kahn. Verlaine and Baudelaire, Maeterlinck, Kahn, and their poetic kind, are, for Mr. Loeffler, as bone of his bone, flesh of his flesh. Their imaginative waywardness, their delicacy of intimation, their preoccupation with the fantastic, are, to him, transcendently appealing; and their distinguishing characteristics find definite analogues in his music. Whether in the brooding terror, the vague and tragic sweetness of his "Tintagiles"; whether in the exquisite and gleaming color of his transmutation of the poem from "La Bonne Chanson," or in the evasive loveliness of the songs, Mr. Loeffler reflects the precise quality and timbre of his poetic subject—reveals them in the light of his own strange and engaging temperament.

It is a suggestive index to his point of approach, and to his powers, that he will touch only refined gold. I do not know that he has ever set a mediocre, a banal poem to music—that he has been concerned with anything less than the excellent; certainly he has written nothing which is not touched with that fine distinction, that rarity of thought, which have given him a place apart in the literature of music. The *clichée* phrase, the outworn formula, the moribund convention, are unaffectedly odious in his sight. His horror of the obvious is as genuine and inveterate as is Meredith's, or Baudelaire's, or Mr. Yeats's. It leads him occasionally, indeed, into what one is tempted to call an extravagance of subtlety; the substance of his inspiration is refined, one feels at times, to the point of attenuation. More often, though, it vitalizes work of extraordinary beauty, of vivid individuality—music that has scarcely its superior, that has, in fact, few equals, for imaginative vision, for originality of contrivance, for insinuating eloquence.

In his musical style Mr. Loeffler has a certain kinship with the school of contemporary France; he is of a kind with Debussy, with Vincent d'Indy, with Fauré, with Pierre de Bréville, and with the dead master, César Franck—the school whose capital traits are finesse, a passion for the recondite, a scrupulous avoidance of too definite, too facile patterns, an exquisite mastery of harmonic and orchestral color. With Mr. Loeffler these traits are a most conspicuous possession. He is, in his artistic constitution, pre - eminently Gallic—so far as the term is a signal for

69

fastidiousness, for dexterity, for sen-
sibility. The overwhelming impact of
Wagner's genius seems, happily, not to
have involved him in any appreciable
degree; what little of the Teutonic
tradition he has inherited is connoted by
occasional touches in his work of a
quality which one knows only in Brahms
—and Brahms, let it be remarked, at his
best, his most admirably Teutonic.

Mr. Loeffler, then, owing something
to the subtlest and most sensitizing
influences in the musical art of to-day,
is himself an influential force of definite
potency. As Mr. Philip Hale has remarked, with acute and just perception, "There are poets who are apart
—Poe, the Thomson of 'The City of
Dreadful Night,' Baudelaire. There
are dramatists of kin, as Tourneur,
Webster, Ford, and Maeterlinck. In
music there is Loeffler." He has given

us an art in which the declaration is of an emotion within emotion, an alembicated eloquence—an eloquence which prevails through its very passivity. But you will not know its spell at once, for its beauty issues from remote and hidden sources.

PIETRO MASCAGNI

WHATEVER a remoter verdict may determine as to Pietro Mascagni's proper place in the history of musical art, it is impossible to-day to escape the conviction that he is, in a very certain and complete degree, the essential musician of the theatre—the consistent lyrico-dramatic commentator of Wagner's unrealized dreams. Wherewith I come to a most curious point of comparison.

It is one of the strangest paradoxes in musical history that Wagner, in attempting a concrete embodiment of his ideal of an uncompromisingly subordinate musico-dramatic speech, should have failed as signally as if he had been, instead of the impassioned follower of Gluck and the Florentines, the most irreclaimable of the Neapolitans. Surely, in the entire range of the arts, there is no case that would seem to make so exquisitely ironic an appeal to the tenderer moods of the Comic Spirit than the amazing spectacle of Wagner the dramatic poet, Wagner the regenerator of the *dramma per musica*, the relentless antagonist of opera for music's sake, producing lyric plays in which the music overshadows the drama as the "Hamlet" of Shakespeare overshadows the "Hamlet" of Tschaikowsky. Wagner, primarily and fundamentally a musical artist, a weaver of tonal spells, must inevitably have defeated his own ends when he undertook to realize his— for him—unattainable ideal of a lyrical drama in which the music should be

merely accessory and contributive. It
was not that he fell short, but that he
went too far: he should have stopped—
as Mascagni stops—at mere intensification. He wrote for his dramas, instead
of music that should have been merely
supplemental and significant, music that
is, in and of itself, so superlative, so
engrossing, so stupendous and exigent in
its beauty, that it becomes the over-
whelmingly dominant and engaging
factor. "Tristan und Isolde" is, as
Ernest Newman has remarked, "not
so much an opera as a symphonic poem
to which words have sometimes been
added, by hook or by crook."

It was a glorious, a triumphant failure
—but a failure, nevertheless, if he were
to stand or fall by his purpose rather
than by his achievement; and where
Wagner, in his "Tristan" and "Meistersinger" and "Parsifal," fails, Mascagni,

in (say) his "Cavalleria Rusticana,"
succeeds. "Cavalleria" is a veritable
music-drama — a rude approximation
of Wagner's conception of a drama
vitalized and emotionally quickened by
a co-operative but subsidiary musical
accompaniment. Here is no absorb-
ingly gorgeous fabric of musical in-
vestiture to divert the attention and the
imagination from the immediate concerns of the drama itself. The music
throughout is almost invariably atten-
dant upon the dramatic action. It is
subservient and reflective; seldom does
it assert itself beyond the limits imposed by its proper function of simply
heightening and intensifying the emotional appeal of the play. It fulfils
admirably, in the main, Wagner's precept that the auditor should be aware
of the music only as an enforcement and
intensification of the dramatic moment.

Here it is precisely that—the naked, the sheer equivalent of the inner and the external movement of the tragedy. That, beyond question, is its excelling virtue: its persistent co-ordination of the action and the tone, its singleness of purpose and effect. In that it is an extraordinary achievement. The music, *quâ* music, has nothing of that tragic beauty which in Wagner's "Götter-dämmerung," for example, entrances the sense and "turns the heart to water"; and to call it distinguished, in any merely musical sense, would be grotesquely to pervert the fact. Its melodic vein is predominantly coarse and obvious; its harmonic plan is wantonly uncouth; its musicianship is unimpressive: but despite its frequent and violent departures from musical rectitude, its vulgarity and extravagance and blatant crudity, the score of "Cavalleria" re-

76

mains a tragic masterpiece, unique in its concision, its swiftness, its unswerving dramatic verity.

"Cavalleria," of course, we had known before Mascagni's personal invasion of our operatic stage,—though his memorably fine interpretation of the score revealed unsuspected and admirable excellences in its structure and effect. But of his other operas we knew only "L'Amico Fritz," a work highly inconsequential and unrepresentative, and of negligible significance in its relation to the development of Mascagni's artistic personality. The composer's visit, however, calamitous and abortive as it was, served to disclose aspects of his art at once surprising and delightful.

The Mascagni of old—the Mascagni of "Cavalleria"—was a man direct and impetuous of utterance almost to the point of brutality,—hot-blooded, vehement, superlatively uncontemplative. The Mascagni of later revelation — the Mascagni of "Zanetto" and "Iris" — is an honest pagan turned would-be mystic, an ineffectual dreamer, a seeker after the distinguished phrase and the subtler inspiration—in short, a talent of uncommon virility and exuberance, widened in scope and shaped to a finer utterance, to a maturer and more heedful poise, but still, in its impulses, unregulated and chaotic.

It is extremely fortunate that Mascagni was enabled to produce his "Iris" here, and that we were not under the necessity of basing a judgment of his later work upon "Zanetto" alone. The text is derived by Mascagni's librettists, Signori Targioni-Tozzetti and Menasci, from François Coppée's delightful idyl, "Le Passant." Silvia, the charming hostess of a country inn, is become

78

blasé and jaded from a life of much
emotional activity.   She encounters
Zanetto, a roving minstrel, for whom she
conceives a sincere passion.   Zanetto,
also enamoured, proffers his devotion;
but Silvia, who has meanwhile been made
aware of an ultimate and transcendent
ideal not to be attained through mere
human tenderness, denies her love and
his, and sends him from her.   And the
moral of it all, the libretto naïvely ex-
plains, "is that true love is willing to
sacrifice itself in order that its ideal
may achieve its high ambition."   In
itself, the little drama has an undeniable
charm.   There is a noble and penetrating aspiration implicit in its central
motive, a high and gracious poetry in its
symbolism.   It is curiously like, in intention, that other and miraculously
lovely spiritual fable, Mr. Yeats's "The
Shadowy Waters."   Silvia is a feminine

79

and sentimentalized Forgæl, become suddenly aware that

> "The love of all under the light of the sun
> Is but brief longing, and deceiving hope,
> And bodily tenderness,"

and denying Zanetto and his humanly eager passion as Forgæl denies Dectora. Here, obviously, is a conception which it is perhaps unreasonable to suppose that such a musician as Mascagni could ever have comprehended; it is inconceivable that he could ever have realized it musically. Peter Cornelius would have contrived an exquisite setting for such a theme; César Franck, or Debussy, or Vincent d'Indy, might have found for it an adequate musical equivalent. But for Mascagni that feat were impossible. Quintessentially Italian, he is anything but a mystic; his temperament is, in fact, at a further

80

remove from the temperament of the typical mystic, the clairvoyant visionary, than that of almost any composer in the history of music. His art knows no hesitancies, no withdrawals into the shadow; whatever of beauty and intensity it owns is of the surface, obvious in the most immediate sense of the word. He is not of that clan who have "turned their longing after the wind and wave of the mind." He is the sheer materialist, untroubled by any too urgent intuitions of the dæmonic, and with no message of any sort—save that of his own gospel of musical beauty—to deliver. Such a temperament, one would have said in advance of the event, could not but be permanently disqualified for the musical expression of such a subject; and so it has proved. The score of "Zanetto" is a miracle of dulness; throughout its dreary length it contains

scarcely a phrase that is not compact
of unrelieved platitude. One waits for
a passion and a poignancy, a moment of
vivifying emotion, that never comes.
There is no heightening, no grasp of
mood, no distinction of style. There
is, in short, a complete and lamentable
absence of inspiration. It was scarcely
to be expected that Mascagni would
achieve spiritual intensity, or any subtlety of interpretation. But here are not
even the vividness and the passion of
"Cavalleria," nor its eloquent brevity
of characterization. "Zanetto" must be
—one most sincerely hopes that it is—
a monument of the lowest ebb to which
it is possible for Mascagni's powers to
decline.

"Iris" is in a wholly different case.
It justifies, in a measure, the faith in
Mascagni's potentialities which "Caval-
leria" inspired, and which European

judgments of his subsequent performances tended so persistently to dis-
courage. One is scarcely prepared to
maintain that in "Iris" he has actually
accomplished all that was promised of
him under the sway of those unheedful
enthusiasms of the early nineties. But
beyond any question at all the music of
"Iris" is the most brilliant, the most
pregnant, the most distinguished that
we have yet heard from Mascagni.
With one's ears haunted by the memory of such a phrase as Cieco's deeply
pathetic "*Una carezza al vecchio Cieco!*"
it is difficult to believe that one has been
listening to music by the composer of
"Zanetto" and—the "Intermezzo."

As a dramatic text, "Iris" is preposterous. A tragic action devoid of
essential humanity, with no logical or-
ganic growth, and crassly melodramatic
in its structure, is framed in a set-

ting of Oriental symbolism superfi-
cially felt and unintelligently utilized,
and bearing merely a decorative relation to the drama. Iris, a young and
guileless Japanese, is abducted by an
adventurous roué and detained against
her will in a resort in the Yoshiwara.
Her blind and decrepit father, believing
that she has deserted him voluntarily,
seeks her out and curses her, flinging
mud in her face. Iris, crazed by his
imprecations, throws herself from a
window into an adjacent sewer, where
she is discovered, half alive, by some
wandering rag - pickers. As the sun
rises she expires, and (in the exalted
phrase of the libretto) "flowers . . .
knot themselves about her, as human
arms, and lift her up towards the
Azure, the Infinite, and to the Sun."
Upon this basis of sheer melodrama and
ineffectual allegory, Mascagni has erect-

ed a musical structure which is, when
one considers the material with which
he had to work, surprisingly effective.
There are moments of labored and
abortive ugliness; the psychology is often
lacking in acuteness, and the invention
not infrequently flags. But, when all
has been said that may justly be
affirmed in depreciation, this impassioned and colorful score still remains a
remarkable achievement. There are notable passages—the sonorous introduction, with its climax of radiant orchestral light; Cieco's agonized lament, and
the conclusion of the first act; Iris's
narrative in the second act; Osaka's
passionate supplications; Iris's dying
soliloquy. Above all—and it is the
redeeming trait of Mascagni's artistic
character, the palliation for his obvious
faults of over-emphasis, and brutality,
and incoherence—there is the constant

presence, in this as in his other works, of that "splendid and imperishable excellence" which Mr. Swinburne found to atone for all of Byron's offences and to outweigh all his defects: "the excellence of sincerity and strength." That much, at least, Mascagni's most grudging detractor must concede to him.

At that time, sufficiently remote from the present, when it will be possible and right to attempt a final estimate of Mascagni, I think it will be said of him that he was primarily a worker in the open, going no further than an immitigable sincerity and an unconquerable enthusiasm could take him—not caring, in fact, to penetrate very deeply or curiously beneath the human surfaces of life. The events of the psychic world—the world of emotion and desire and passionate conflict—dominate his imagination and completely enchain his spirit. He has not "a far-wandering wing"; nor has he the remotest concern with that otherworld "on whose leaning brows are mystery and shadow." Not for him the troubled and eager quest of that inexorable ideal which offers "but wind and shadow" for reward in the attainment; nor, for him, the unwearying search for an ultimate beauty, a perfected design and utterance. But whatever virtues inhabit sincerity and truth and power are his, beyond the possibility of denial.

A NOTE ON GRIEG

It is the habit of musicians of a
certain stamp to speak of Edvard
Grieg with a slightly contemptuous lift-
ing of the brows—an artist, they will
concede, of charming and distinguished
accomplishment, but restricted in scope
and power. A popular legend accounts
him to be peculiarly a master of the
exotic, uttering a beauty essentially
slight and rare, remote and exquisitely
fantastic, rather than broadly virile and
of deep emotional significance. "Grieg,"
one may read in a recent and deliberate
estimate of the Norwegian's genius,
"is never large or heroic; he never wears
the buskin. He has neither the depth

of passion nor the intellectual grasp needed to make music in the grand style." His personality, we are told, is one "graceful without strength, romantic without the sense of tragedy, highly gifted with all gentle qualities of nature, but lacking in the more virile powers, in broad vision, epic magnanimity, and massive force"—a conception of his genius which one need have no hesitation in declaring superficial and incomplete. Grieg is not merely gracious and fragrant, piquant and fragilely lovely; he is all this, of course, but he is very much more: he is also a poet of the tragic, of the largely passionate and elemental.

Let me, in bearing brief witness to a side of his genius that is seldom insisted upon, allege several definite points of evidence. Consider, for a moment, that work of his in which he reached, perhaps, the highest point to which his power of creative genius can take him—the sonata for violin and piano in C minor, Op. 45. Here, in my view, is a work built greatly upon great lines. I find in it no hint of the limitations which that dubious appraiser of Grieg whom I have quoted discovers in the work of the Norwegian. The mood, the emotion, are heroic; here are virility, breadth, a passionate urge and ardor. With what an intensity of grieving Grieg has charged those wailing chromatic phrases, for the violin and piano in imitation, in the working-out section of the first movement! and the C major passage in the last movement, with its richly canorous theme for the solo instrument against arching arpeggios in the accompaniment, is superb in breadth and power.

Then, again, there is the "Aase's

Tod," from the first Peer Gynt Suite—
a threnody of sombre and obsessing
beauty, large in conception, noble and
profound in feeling,—the product of
a temperament rich in capacity and
resource. I might allege, too, many of
the songs—"Friendship," for example;
or the magnificent G minor Ballade,
Op. 24; or the "Bergliot" music, or
portions of "Olav Trygvason."

I have not the smallest intention of
denying the existence of the Grieg of
popular tradition. He is, at times, simply and contentedly, one of the minor
singers; or he tells us only, in the fortunate phrase of Mr. Philip Hale, of
"elves" who "hardly thumb-high, play
as *succubi* and *incubi*"; or of elves "who
wear the face of a fresh and adorable
virgin—yet they borrow only half of a
human body, and they do not turn their
backs; because if they were to do this,

one could see that they are hollow behind, like a mask." That is, indeed,
Grieg—the slighter Grieg; but what of
the other Grieg—the Grieg of "Olav"
and "Bergliot"? to whom Mr. Hale has
himself applied the memorable and
majestic lines of Walt Whitman:

"I see the burial cairns of Scandinavian
warriors; I see them raised high with stones,
by the marge of restless oceans, that the dead
men's spirits, when they wearied of their quiet
graves, might rise up through the mounds,
and gaze on the tossing billows, and be
refreshed by storms, immensity, liberty,
action."

Here is no dainty romanticist, no frail
and lovely dreamer; the voice is the
voice of a master of emotional utterance
—here are passion, and pathos, and
heroic ecstasy and despair: here, in
short, is a music-maker whose place is
not, indeed, upon the summit, but certainly upon the upper slopes.

WOMEN AND MODERN MUSIC

THAT most lively and inquisitive of musical essayists, Mr. James Huneker, once speculated with sanity and penetration upon the subject of woman's place in interpretative music. After suggesting, through a felicitously chosen passage from Balzac, the quality of eloquence which he believed to be the extent of feminine accomplishment in piano-playing, Mr. Huneker closed upon this rather dubious note: "It is often charming [a woman's version of Bach, Beethoven, and Brahms], but is it ever great, spiritual, moving art?" Mr. Huneker discreetly forbore to answer his own query, although he implied his

93

conviction unmistakably enough in the shaping of his interrogation.

Let me extend the scope of his inquiry and ask if woman has ever done greatly in creative musical art? Indisputably she has not; we have had no feminine Bach or Wagner—nor even a feminine Dvořák or Puccini. But, one comes to wonder, is woman capable of great creative achievement in this most sensitive, pliant, and emotional of the arts? Frankly, there is everything to warrant the conviction that she is not. Mr. Havelock Ellis, a brilliant and acute psychologist, endorses the view that Mr. G. P. Upton takes of the matter in his *Woman and Music*. Conceding, says Mr. Upton, that music is the most intense and potent medium for the expression of the emotions, and that woman is emotional by nature, "is it not one solution of the problem that

94

woman does not musically reproduce them because she herself is emotional by temperament and nature and cannot project herself outwardly? . . . The emotion is a part of herself and is as natural to her as breathing. She lives in emotion and acts from emotion; . . . but to treat emotions as if they were mathematics, to bind and measure and limit them within the rigid laws of harmony and counterpoint, and to express them with arbitrary signs, is a cold-blooded operation possible only to the sterner and more obdurate nature of man." All of which is exceedingly convincing and explanatory. Women have wrought admirably, at times incomparably, in letters—witness, for an example of to-day, the marvellously lovely and moving art of that exquisite genius, Fiona Macleod; and in painting they have worked to honorable ends;

95

but what woman has written music that
is to be mentioned in the same breath
with the work of George Eliot, of
Christina Rossetti, of Mrs. Browning, of
Rosa Bonheur, of Nora Hopper and
Miss Macleod? Surely not Clara Schumann, nor Augusta Holmes, nor the in-
corrigibly superficial Chaminade, nor
such accomplished and earnest music-
makers as those ambitious Americans,
Mrs. H. H. A. Beach and Miss Margaret
Ruthven Lang—to name those among
the most eminent who come first to mind.

It has been urged that the woman
composer has had, as yet, scarcely a
chance—in Mr. Kipling's convenient
phrase—to "find herself"; but it will
be conceded that she has had at least
equal opportunities with her sisters in
literature and art. Certainly there are
to-day no insurmountable obstacles in
her path: for a contemporary composer

96

has proved that it is possible for a woman to compass the amazing feat of achieving the production of an original opera at that august temple of the lyric muse—the Metropolitan Opera-House. When Miss Ethel M. Smyth bowed her acknowledgments from a be-flowered stage after the curtain had fallen upon the final scene of her music-drama, "Der Wald," she marked the consummation of a unique accomplish-ment—never before in the history of American music had an opera by a woman been publicly performed; it re-mained for an Englishwoman—though with Teutonic affiliations—to effect that unexampled end. And are we to say that so extraordinary a success justified itself through the disclosure of any singular gift of genius? It would be difficult to say so save in a spirit of the most desperate and defiant gallantry.

Another explanation of feminine incapacity in this field—at best, I admit, a partial one—suggests itself.

Would one be guilty of an inclination toward the fantastical in postulating—with a proper tentativeness — that almost all great modern music has been inspired, in variable degree, by the ideal of sex—an ideal that has necessarily, for the masculine composer, been feminine? The most intense and eloquent music we have was written as an idealized expression of sexual love. Think of the D minor symphony of Schumann, certain songs of Schubert and Brahms, the supreme passages in the music dramas of Wagner —would they have been possible without the stimulus of some personal ideal of feminine loveliness? Women did not begin to compete with men in the field of composition, to any extent, until music had ceased to be merely decorative or religious, as it was, predominantly, before Beethoven's time, and had begun to serve as a medium for emotional expression; therefore there was little opportunity for the development of a female Bach or Haydn. So it happened that when women did begin to turn their attention to the writing of music they found it an art which was essentially a vehicle of expression, and only incidentally an art of formal beauty. What was it, then, that was lacking in the equipment of the woman composer that interfered with her producing music of veritable power and intensity? Is it not fair to suppose that it was, in large part, the lack of that urgent inspiration which she herself furnishes to her brother composer? Obviously the ideal of masculine personality does not occupy a place in women's imaginations analogous with the ideal of feminine personality which fires and stimulates the imaginations of men; for, to the masculine mind, ideal beauty—the governing motive in the inspiration of creative work—presents itself generally in terms of a perfected feminine loveliness: an identification which does not, of course, exist for women in any corresponding relationship.

Look deep enough into almost any of the great modern scores penned by men and you will find, however reconditely, the image of a woman's face. Look into any score of feminine authorship and you will find a "painted idyl of what never was." And would you set this flaccid simulation against such a transcendent utterance of the heart's desire, such a " dream of the enchanted spirit of man, achieved in beauty," as "Tristan und Isolde"?

WOMEN AND MODERN MUSIC

"It is woman who [as an inspirational force] composes all the great music, paints all the great pictures, writes all the great poems," says the author of "Overtones." That is, perhaps, too wide an extension of the theory; but of music it goes to the heart of the matter.

A REJECTED MUSIC-DRAMA

His detractors would say that the first American production of Mr. Isidore de Lara's music-drama, "Messaline," in the winter of 1902, was chiefly notable in that it evoked probably the most emphatic and unequivocal condemnation that had ever greeted the *première* of a new work in this country. The shortest of memories must concede the fact. Yet—and I would note here that he is a temerous appraiser who ventures to set any value whatsoever upon "Messaline"—yet, I say, a critic would surely be deserving of scant confidence were he not to testify, at whatever risk of error, to that in a work of creative art which may seem to himself imperative in excellence. I can only say, therefore, that Mr. de Lara's lyric tragedy seems to me, after a matured familiarity with it, to be a work of remarkable, though unsustained, beauty, and of very considerable intensity.

For the effectiveness of many of his scenes Mr. de Lara is, beyond a doubt, deeply indebted to the admirable libretto of his collaborators, Messrs. Sylvestre and Morand; for his music is usually abortive when it attempts to realize a supremely tragic situation — such, for example, as the conclusion of the second act, with Harès's agonized "*Elle! grands dieux! c'est elle! et dans ses bras!*" or the tremendous final scene at the end of the last act. In such moments as these it is the dexterous dramatic contrivance, rather than the accompanying music, which works so poignant and overmastering an effect. Mr. de Lara's inspiration sinks at such times to its lowest ebb. It is when his librettists afford him an occasion for giving the most unrestrained play to his lyric emotion and his gift of majestic expression that he rises to his fullest height. One cannot soon forget moments in the opening chorus, nor the music at Messaline's entrance, nor the love scene between herself and Harès, nor the greater part of the third act. Above all, De Lara has realized musically the character of Messaline with an astonishing subtlety, an astonishing intensity, vitality, and puissance. He has painted her to the life, this most magnificent of courtesans. Not only has he vivified the actual Messaline, as Messrs. Sylvestre and Morand have recreated her, but she becomes in his music the type and embodiment of the essential, the supreme enchantress, the seductress of immemorial incarnations. Nowhere is he happier, more brilliantly compelling, than in his delineation of her moods—or, rather, her mood, for she has but one, although she plays upon it manifold and incalculable variations;—and at that passage in her love scene with Harès where, as Calvé enacts her, she rises from her silver couch to caress her still timorous lover, while her most original and haunting motive broadens with lingering tenderness in the orchestra, one feels that here, at least, De Lara has actually accomplished an exquisite piece of musical psychologizing, and one rejoices. For it is only in his characterization of Messaline herself that he succeeds in quite convincing us. His Hélion is, if one must say it, almost a failure, so far as his credible existence in the score is concerned. And

in this, too, De Lara falls short of his
text for persuasive dramatic power.
His Harès is better, although one must
rebel at the "*O nuit d'amour*" in the
tavern scene, which is sheer Tosti—the
one egregious blot upon Mr. de Lara's
score.

Another blot, though a lesser one,
is his irritating predilection for the
perfect cadence. He not infrequently chooses to interrupt the surge and
flow of his larger orchestral movement
for the sake, so it would seem, of a
concluding high note. Nor—to continue
this catalogue of his imperfections—
are his declamatory passages especially
memorable. He has not sufficient harmonic pregnancy to support his recita-
tives with a rich and significant current
of orchestral commentary. In fact, his
orchestra is rather dependent than
emancipated, in the modern musico-

dramatic sense. Mr. de Lara restricts it, in the main, merely to sustaining his voice parts, although his manipulation of the few motives that the score contains is often extremely effective; particularly so is his use of Messaline's typical theme and the several beautiful love motives.

If I were called upon to attempt a sudden summing up of "Messaline," I should say that, regarded simply from the point of view of dramatic workmanship, it is strikingly successful; that, musically, leaving the text aside, its poignant lyricism saves it at times from declining into something dangerously like banality; and that, in its exposition of the character of Messaline herself, the score is nothing short of masterly.

Into the perilous and unprofitable question of the morals of Mr. de Lara's opera I am not in the least inclined to enter exhaustively. But if I considered it incumbent upon me to debate the ethical point involved, I should emphatically hold that " Messaline," far from being merely an offensive and deleterious chronicle of lust and infamy, is essentially an exhortation against sexual depravity. With Mr. Vernon Blackburn, I " can quite imagine ' Messaline ' being taken by any serious and zealous pastor as a text whereon to hang the most significant of sermons, as a classic instance wherewith to point his moral and adorn his tale." For, as Mr. Blackburn justly contends, " here is no triumph of sin. The cautionary tales themselves do not hold a more complete record of the punishment assigned to lawlessness and self-indulgence." I can find no more conclusive word to say on the subject than that.

THE QUESTION OF REALISM

PROGRAM-MUSIC, we have been told
repeatedly by unimpeachable authori-
ties, attains artistic respectability only
when and so long as it contents itself with
suggesting and enforcing a poetic mood
or ideal; when it becomes imitative of
externals (they say) it courts degradation.—Thus runs the dictum, so strenu-
ously maintained by generations of val-
iant feuilletonists. Imitative music is
the black sheep, the shameless outcast
of the art. When you have said of
a composer's music that it is "merely
imitative," you have pronounced judgment of excommunication; denunciation
can go no further.

Mr. W. J. Henderson, in a sentence in his admirable essay on Schumann and the program-symphony, has afforded me a kind of inverted text for this discourse. "Sometimes," he says, "in the carrying out of a great plan, the masters have written music designed to conjure up in the mind images of external objects; but to do this is to put music to its lowest use." And hear Mr. Frederick Corder, in his Grove's Dictionary article on program - music: ". . . it is a degradation of art to employ music in imitating the sounds of nature."

Now, if I may venture to differ with Mr. Henderson and Mr. Corder, it is precisely because the masters have done this very thing, — flagrantly, often, and to the glory of art, — that imitative tone-painting has an established right to be considered a legitimate

form of musical expression. Certainly
it is irrefragable that some of the most
beautiful and poetic music in existence
is frankly designed to induce images of
external things. Numerous desperate
attempts have been made to palliate the
arrant realism of the "Siegfried" Wald-
weben, for instance (one naturally turns
to Wagner, as the great master of descriptive music, for illustrations); but
any one who can listen without prejudice
to that lovely episode and affirm that it
is anything but sheer musical scene-
painting, is simply denying the obvious.
If you have a theoretical axe to grind,
and are trying to square this particular
scene with some complacently orthodox
theory of musical ethics, you may ex-
plain that Wagner is aiming to translate
a psychic mood, that he is merely in-
terpreting Siegfried's emotional impressions; you may assert this, but how will

you account for those delicious and unmistakable orchestral bird songs—as unmistakable as the avian warblings in the andante of the " Pastoral Symphony "—and the barefaced attempts to picture the rustling and shimmering of leaves and the play of sunlight? So far as Wagner is concerned, it is unnecessary to multiply examples; a dozen others are readily recallable: the gorgeous musical. tumult which describes Siegfried's ascent of Brünnhilde's flame-girdled rock; the "Walküre" fire-music; the "Rheingold" prelude and finale; the exquisite orchestral commentary which accompanies Isolde's rhapsodizing at the beginning of the second act of "Tristan" —"Sie winkt mit einem Tuche," writes Wagner, in his stage directions, near the end of the scene; and out of the figure which he invents to accompany the action he makes a page of ravishing musical loveliness. Surely this is imitative music at its worst!

It need hardly be said, though, that it is unnecessary to look to the music-drama for examples of realistic descriptive music which is, in itself, as beautiful as it is dignified. To come directly to Beethoven, the "Pastoral Symphony" immediately suggests itself, of course, as a thoroughly admirable example of objective tone - painting. Although it has been defended by timorous apologists, and in spite of its deprecatory motto, I think it will be conceded by impartial critics that in it Beethoven has concerned himself rather more with "Malerei" than with "Ausdruck der Empfindung." Ambros speaks of the first movement as "a broad landscape - picture"; and it is not easy to see that, in the matter of its intention, the "Thunderstorm" varies in any essential particular from other musical storms of a less exalted reputation. Mr. George P. Upton finds in it all the familiar properties of the symphonic storm: it "brings before us the lowering sky, the distant rumbling of thunder, the sultry air, and the cumulous clouds as they rise higher and higher above the horizon, until we are almost in darkness, and the storm breaks forth in all its fury. It soon passes over, however, and sunlight illuminates the refreshed landscape," etc. It is only by virtue of the intrinsic dignity of its musical investment that it ranks as a work of art instead of as a piece of pretentious clap-trap.

Mendelssohn, who can scarcely be accused of a contempt for the canons of musical respectability, has made familiarly successful and charming use of imitative music in his "Midsummer Night's Dream" score. Berlioz, Liszt,

Rubinstein, Raff, Goldmark, Elgar,
Rimsky - Korsakoff, Rachmaninoff, are
some who should also be remembered
in the indictment. Saint - Saëns, too,
temperamental classicist as he is, has
yet made audacious and notable experi-
ments in delineative music. In that
most vivacious of his symphonic poems,
"Phaéton," the details of the intrepid
charioteer's mad adventure are de-
scribed with graphic effect and fine
poetic gusto. Mr. Upton, in a picturesque and sprightly analysis, thus inter-
prets the climax: "At last," he says,
"Jupiter settles matters with an out-
burst of trumpets"—this, though, Mr.
Upton might depose, should justly be
regarded as the enforcement of a mood;
but the important point to note is, that
this turbulent tone-picture of streaming
manes, and motion, and light, is excellent
music—the themes succinct and virile,

the architecture adroit and firm, the conception large and imaginative.

Then there is Richard Strauss—that egregious stumbling-block to the decorous and the law-abiding—who, in those colossal and brilliant phantasmagorias of his, "Till Eulenspiegel," "Don Quixote," and (in parts) "Also Sprach Zarathustra," has achieved stupendous and overmastering effects by methods which are the reverse of idealistic. Edward MacDowell's "The Eagle"—an illustration to Tennyson's lines—is another example (there are innumerable ones that might be adduced) of finely imaginative tone-painting. It aims to arouse, through the potency of various musical devices, the same succession of mental pictures which is induced by the words of the poem, each image having its counterpart in the music. A depiction of

116

externals it indubitably is; but where
are your scruples in face of the impressiveness of the musical result? Which
brings one to the point to be em-
phasized—in the form of a proposition
so self - evident that it seems hardly
worth setting down:—namely, that in
music, as in the other arts, the product, the achievement, is everything; the
means count for nothing. If, by the
use of a descriptive process of any sort,
even the most closely realistic, a composer is enabled to contrive music
which is poetic, vital, thematically
original—if, in short, it stands the test
of a purely musical standard of valuation, and so long as it conveys no
strabismic view of life or the natural
world, he has created an art-work whose
legitimacy is, it would seem, theoretical-
ly unquestionable. It is difficult to see
that the fact of his having chosen to

represent musically an externality—
which does not, of course, preclude
artistic selection and accentuation—
involves any degradation, any prostitu-
tion of the art, as we are assured that
it does. "The solitary question to ask
of a new composition," wrote Sidney
Lanier, "is—not, is it descriptive, but
is it beautiful in any, the largest sense
of that term?" And Schumann's
"nothing is wrong in music which sounds
right" can bear the strain of a wider
application than is usually given it.
Lanier (to quote him again) wrote
appositely in connection with the "Pastoral Symphony," in his *Poetry and
Music:* "Beethoven wishes to suggest
a definite intellectual image to his
hearers along with a certain set of tones;
instead of employing a conventional
word to accomplish his purpose he
chooses to employ an imitative tone.

Nothing could be more natural, nothing more legitimate. Why not hint a storm with stormy tones as well as describe a storm in stormy words?"

It is simply a question of ideation (if one may use the word in a musical sense): one man—an artist, endowed with poetic insight—will set out to express in music the ripple of water, the pounding of horses' hoofs, the swirl and turmoil of a gale at sea,—any one of the familiar phenomena beloved of the musical realist; another, barren of sentiment and imagination, attempts the same thing: the difference in result will be as the difference between a still-life by Vollon and a still-life by any one else. That the basis of both is imitation, an endeavor "to conjure up in the mind images of external objects," has no logical bearing whatever on the case; the quality of the translation, as music, is the only consideration which should weigh in the appraisement. Iamblichus—neo-Platonist, mathematician, and musical theorist—summed up the matter with notable terseness some sixteen centuries ago. "Things more excellent than every image," he wrote, "are expressed through images."

Wagner, his flamboyant realism transformed and sublimated by the surpassing eloquence of its musical embodiment, stands for the perfect type of the descriptive painter in tones. His transmutation—imitation, if you prefer —of the multitudinous sounds and aspects of the external world is recorded in page after page of music which is its own superb and triumphant justification.

A NEGLECTED SONG WRITER

A QUARTER of a century before that flaunting signature of musical modernity, "Ein Heldenleben," issued from the hand of Richard Strauss, there died in Germany a composer whose significant work is to-day as fresh and modern, as contemporary in its impulse and address, as any music whose origin is of the present. With the outward life of Peter Cornelius I shall not here concern myself. A nephew of the painter Von Cornelius, he was a friend and protégé of Liszt, an early propagandist for the Wagner cause, a writer upon music, a teacher, at one time an actor—that, in the briefest outline, is the substance of the biographies. He lived out his life during a period of the most consuming and momentous activity in the development of the art to whose service his career was a devotion; and yet, somehow, he found opportunity and inspiration for the writing of songs steeped in a loveliness whose serenity and detachment have scarcely, in music, an adducible parallel. There, I conceive, is the curiosity.

Neglected, I have called him, and in no mere mood of inconsiderate and impetuous sympathy. The world at large knows him only as the author of a delightful comedy—"Der Barbier von Bagdad," of some admirable choral music, and, virtually, of a single song— the ubiquitous and lovely "Ein Ton." One will look in vain through the pages of Mr. Henry T. Finck's excellent and appreciative *Songs and Song*

122

Writers for any mention of his work—
an omission which it is not easy to
justify when one considers, not alone the
quality of Cornelius's genius, but the
quite substantial bulk of his output.

And yet it is not, perhaps, so inex-
plicable as it seems at first blush that
his songs should be—except, to a limited
extent, in Germany — practically un-
known and unsung; for Cornelius be-
longs, with such others as Fiona Macleod
and George Russell and Charles Martin
Loeffler, to that distinguished minority
of undemonstrative geniuses whose
voices have never penetrated to the ears
of the many—whose utterances have
been too rare, too subtly graduated, too
little insistent, to arrest the attention of
those who give heed only to the inescapable. Cornelius never ·takes one
by storm. He has, veritably enough,
as Mr. Meredith postulates of his figure

of an Egoist, the gift of pathos—only he does not "rush at you, roll you over, and squeeze your body for the briny drops." He is insuperably, confirmedly undramatic. His is not the way of the scenic imagination, the method which relies upon the challenging appeal of sudden contrast, of emotion set in vivid relief against emotion. One would search fruitlessly through his work for a song of the order of Schubert's "Der Doppelgänger," or Tschaikowsky's "Warum sind denn die Rosen so blass?" —the text of which Cornelius has himself used in a song—or Richard Strauss's "Cäcilie." His appeal is subtle, lingering, intimate, rather than instant and overwhelming. Swiftness, exuberance, passionate emphasis are foreign to his temperament. His is an emotion less impetuous and stressful than contemplative, a passion less expansive

124

than interior: the passion of César Franck rather than of Tschaikowsky, of Yeats rather than of Swinburne—rapt, almost devotional in its moods, and yet tense, compelling, indescribably affecting. His songs, psychic dramas in miniature, are, as Fiona Macleod has written of the plays of Mr. Yeats, "gossamer dramas, woven inwardly of the wind of the spirit and the light of the imagination"; and Cornelius too, at times, "thinks in light and dreams in shadow."

His published songs number, in all, something under threescore: a group of twenty-one,—including the six "Kleine Lieder" and the cyclus "Trauer und Trost,"—three duets for soprano and barytone, six "Weihnachtslieder," four "Lieder für Tenor oder Sopran," six "Brautlieder," three "Sonnette" after Bürger, and fourteen posthumous songs compiled by Max Hasse from Cornelius's sketch - books. Of these fifty-six songs it would scarcely be an extravagance to say that one-half are wholly unimportant—perfunctory, ineffectual, discouragingly uninspired; but the rest are invaluable. It is a sufficiently grievous thing that Cornelius should have permitted himself to write, for instance, his "Im Lenz"— that it is possible to find in the same collection such a perfect thing as "An den Traum" and such a triumph of banality as "Trost." But, after all, was it not possible for the man who could write "Der Tod und das Mädchen" to write also, presumably with a tranquil conscience, "Trockne Blumen"? and did not the author of "The Daffodils" and the "Immortality" ode leave us that perturbing bequest, the "Ecclesiastical Sonnets"? That Cornelius has given

126

us "An den Traum" is, after all, the memorable fact.

His is a personality curiously unsusceptible of definition. He is, when one comes to scrutinize his spirit, bafflingly, illusively complex — an odd comminglement of naïve candor and emotional subtlety. One looks, as it were, into the clear, wide eyes of a child; and then, even as one looks, the eyes alter — they are no longer lucent and untroubled; it is no longer a blithe child, but a dreamer and mystic who gazes back at you through eyes that are become impenetrable and rapt. His thought is, at its most distinctive, tenuous, esoteric, exquisitely reticent —reticent, and yet, as I have said, singularly naïve, singularly buoyant. His world, as we see it through the dim veiling of his music, is a world shut away by a luminous, Corot-like haze, a

world of ineffable and melancholy twi-
light, remote, mysterious, dream-haunted. He is continually obsessed by vague,
tremulous, half - realized visions and
images, heritages of an immemorial
beauty and passion. There are moments when he seems immeasurably
distant, wrapped in a shimmering,
impenetrable mist of dreams; but even
as you would strain your senses to
follow him, he is standing beside you
again, smiling that infinitely winsome
smile of his, and talking to you, with
the most charming naïveté, of fauns, and
butterflies, and Christmas festivals.

It is his unique and perpetual charm
—that curious union of penetrating
mysticism and artless innocence which
is, in poetic art, so pre-eminently
characteristic of William Blake. Cornelius, indeed, reminds one more than
occasionally of Blake in his essential

128

purity and height and sweetness, and in his moods of rapt, ecstatic vision. One may not, however, extend the comparison very far; for Cornelius has abundantly what Blake has not at all: sincere humanity, a clairvoyant and tender intuition of the near, the familiar, the preciously commonplace. Those songs which most justly represent him —such things as "Angedenken," "Trauer," "Ein Ton," "An den Traum," "Nachts," "Auftrag," the "Brautlieder" and "Weihnachtslieder"—are the articulate and surviving documents of one to whom, "upon the public ways, Life came." He has not told us all that, perhaps, he might have told us; but it is something to have borne witness, as he indubitably has, to so much that is of an enduring validity and beauty.

VERDI AND WAGNER:
AN INQUIRY

Now that Giuseppe Verdi has, in Lamb's whimsical phrase, "paid his final tribute to nature," and since an interval sufficient for dispassionate meditation upon the fruits of his existence has elapsed, an attempt to measure his genius, at its essential points, with that of his great contemporary, Wagner, may not seem to lack justification.

I have no wish to touch, in any seemingly wanton spirit, the rim of a controversy which is in nothing so striking as in its futility—the discussion as to the degree of Verdi's indebtedness to Wagner in the matter of precept and

example; but since the point has a
certain initial pertinence in such an ex-
amination as this, the question is not
altogether negligible. That Verdi, then
—the later Verdi of "Aïda," "Otello,"
and "Falstaff" — derived, honorably,
from Wagner, is one of those perfectly
obvious facts in dispute of which con-
troversies occasionally arise. It seems
scarcely worth while to maintain, as is
the habit in certain critical quarters,
that the amazing metamorphosis involved in the writing of "Aïda" and
"Otello" by the composer of "Il Trovatore" was simply the result of spontaneous artistic development—"one of
the grand and gradual processes of
nature," in the imposing phrase of a
certain Verdian biographer. "The step
from 'Il Trovatore' to 'Otello,'" point-
edly observes Mr. Vernon Blackburn,
commenting upon this phenomenon,

"has no parallel in the history of music. It is a development outside all law, all anticipation, all likelihood. The reasonableness for the composition of the first were proof-charge, it might be said in exaggeration, against the reasonableness for the composition of the second, and the history of the human mind bears everywhere a contrary witness to this solitary achievement." It has been averred, in an attempt to account for his extraordinary change of front, that the portents of Verdi's ultimate regeneration are prefigured, to the discerning mind, in the crude and meretricious works of his first and second periods—in "Ernani," "Rigoletto," and "Il Trovatore." In "Rigoletto" especially, Mr. James Huneker finds "the roots of the mature Verdi." "In the declamatory monologues of the hunchback jester," he affirms, "are the germs

132

of the more intellectual and subtle
monologues of Iago and Falstaffo." It
is impossible to quarrel with that; but
the fact surely fails, it must be ad-
mitted, to account for the enormous
disparity between the Verdi of 1867—
the unreclaimed Verdi of "Don Carlos,"
the last work of his second or "transi-
tion" period—and the regenerate Verdi
of 1871, of "Aïda": the Verdi who has
suddenly seen a great light. To find
an adequate and, I think, an entirely
satisfying explanation of so incredible
a development, one has only to recall
the circumstance that, at about this
period of Verdi's career, Richard Wagner was agitating the musical world
with his iconoclastic preachments concerning opera and drama, and that
Verdi, with his undeniable bias towards
musical right-thinking, could scarcely
have helped being powerfully influenced

thereby. "He was quick to perceive," remarks Mr. Blackburn, "the value of the proper Wagnerian reaction which had come; quick to perceive it, quick to utilize it. . . . For not as he sowed did Verdi reap; rather some of the fruit of the seed that Wagner scattered Verdi harvested and gathered into beautiful garners." One may argue thus without in the least implying, it need scarcely be said, that Verdi subserviently patterned his later operas upon Wagnerian lines, or that his inspiration, his point of view, were ever anything but his own. For even though Verdi did profit richly through a sympathetic absorption of Wagner's theories of musico-dramatic art, his application of those theories to his own work was so intensely individual, so intensely and fundamentally Italian, that the question of his derivation of them is important only in so far as it bears upon the estimate, from the historic stand-point, of his total achievement.

It is evident, then (may I say?), at the start, that Verdi was in no sense the original and epoch-making musician that Wagner was. As Mr. Huneker admits, he "was not by nature a reformer." He has been lauded for his conversion; for his unhesitating abandonment of unworthy ideals; for his intelligent and unequivocal adoption of principles wholly antipodal to those he had previously held (if it can be truthfully said that he had formerly held any principles whatsoever). But, admirable as his emancipation must always seem, one's enthusiasm in contemplating it is somewhat qualified by the reflection that it was not, as in Wagner's case, self-sprung. Wagner, in his invincible progress from "Rienzi" to "Tristan und

Isolde," wrought out his own salvation,
despite his primary debt to Weber and
Gluck and the Florentine reformers of
the sixteenth century. But Wagner's
regeneration was truly, as the historian
whom I have quoted said of Verdi, "one
of the grand and gradual processes of
nature"—a matter, certainly, of intellection, but still more of inward necessity,
of intuition, almost, one might say, of
inspiration. With Verdi, on the contrary, the event was as sudden as it was
fortuitous; there is nothing in his earlier
works to account satisfactorily for
"Aïda" and "Otello," and it is impossible to believe that he could have
written them if Wagner had not lived.
Mr. Huneker fathers the ingenious sug-
gestion that, if Verdi was affected at
all by Wagnerism, he was affected not
directly, but by way of Arrigo Boito;
he even hints that Boito had a hand in

the actual writing of "Otello" and
"Falstaff" (a notion which certainly
has an engaging plausibility). But
whether or not Verdi ever heard entire
performances of the "Ring," "Tristan,"
or "Meistersinger"—which Mr. Huneker doubts—is obviously beside the
point. The Wagnerian dialectic was,
so to speak, in the air: its contagion
was inescapable for any one receptively
inclined towards it; and Verdi, with his
predisposition towards musical enlightenment, was unquestionably so inclined.

Viewed, as it were, extra-historically,
and as a musical dramatist *per se*,
Verdi was undeniably a genius of commanding and splendid power (I speak
throughout, of course, of the later and
great Verdi, the Verdi of "Aïda,"
"Otello," and "Falstaff")—"the greatest poet of passion born to Italy," is Mr.
Huneker's just verdict upon him. A

just verdict—yet one that connotes, to my sense, his most conspicuous limitation; since it is only when one comes to measure the expressional efficiency of his music with that of such a master of emotional utterance as Wagner that one realizes its failure to achieve supreme eloquence of accent; for it is in this— in the range and power of his music as an agent of emotional expression, rather than in his achievements as a musical dramatist—that Wagner's greatness essentially consists.

Let me define the measure of comparison somewhat more explicitly.

It is doubtful if any figure in the history of musical art has so continually dwelt in the shadow of misconception and misrepresentation as the poet-composer who imagined a "Ring des Nibelungen," a "Tristan und Isolde," and a "Parsifal." Partly through an

unaccountable popular obtuseness, and
largely through his theoretical pro-
fessions, he has been blindly accepted
at his own fantastic valuation: as a
dramatist who was only incidentally a
musician, as an admirable poet—as anything, in short, save that which he pre-
eminently and paramountly was: a transcendent musician, a profound humanist,
an inspired, but unconscious, mystic.
In his own view, ironically enough, as
in that of the majority of his commentators, his music is simply and solely
the handmaid of his dramatic invention
—simply and solely, as we have been so
carefully instructed, a kind of modern
variant of the exegetical chorus of the
Greek plays. To a certain superficial
extent it is, of course, that; but its
ultimate excellence, its ultimate and
inestimable value, inheres, not—as Wagner fancied, as so many of his disciples

have fancied—in its dramatic apposite-
ness, but in its miraculous range and
eloquence as an instrument of abstract
emotional utterance. For in his endeavor vividly to heighten and in-
tensify every moment of his dramatic
psychologizing, he voiced (almost, one is
tempted to say, accidentally), with
incredible beauty and poignancy, every
elemental mood of the human soul. To
follow him, page by page, through the
score of "Tristan," of "Siegfried," of
"Götterdämmerung," of "Meistersinger," of "Parsifal," is to stand
amazed at the transcendent genius of
this composer whose music—one can
say it in all sobriety—sounds the entire
gamut of human emotion: every note
of passion, of desire, of grief, of terror,
of pity, of delight, of aspiration. His
range is universal: "his lyre has all the
chords."

It is in this — in the perfection and
universality of his expression — that
Wagner is unique and unapproachable;
and it is in this, conversely, that Verdi's
genius falls short of complete accomplishment. As a contrast in sheer
vividness of expression, consider, say,
Verdi's treatment of the scene of
Otello's farewell in comparison with
Wagner's enforcement of a scene psychic-
ally similar — Siegfried's dying apos-
trophe to Brünnhilde. The emotion is
fundamentally the same in both in-
stances, and yet what a striking difference in the exposition of it! Verdi's
is sincere, tense, admirably contrived,
undeniably affecting. Wagner's is overwhelming. Again, to cite but a single
work of Wagner's (though it is, indeed,
the supreme signal of his genius), I
know of nothing in Verdi to parallel
the ineffable longing of Tristan's "Ach,

Isolde!" or the passion of the stupendous C major introductory section of the love duo in the second act, or the anguish of Isolde's "Nur einmal, ach! nur einmal noch!" or the divine ecstasy of the "Liebestod." That Verdi has his unforgettable moments—moments when he utters an emotion with resistless intensity and effect — may be unhesitatingly conceded. In "Aïda," notably, there are passages superb in forcefulness and felicity: such things as the scene of Rhadames' trial by the priests, in the fourth act, interrupted by the agonized interjections of Amneris—the expression which Verdi has found for those sobbing ejaculations could not easily be bettered. Thrice - admirable, too, is Aïda's nostalgic lament in act three: "O patria! O patria! quanto mi costi!" But with Verdi such things are exceptional; his habitual level of inspiration and achievement is very appreciably lower. With Wagner, on the contrary, vividness is of the very fibre and texture of his music; superlatively eloquent expression is as native to his genius, is, with him, as pre-eminently a matter of habit, as, with other composers, it is a matter of occasion.

As Verdi's range of expression is limited, and his expression itself — his expression of any particular mood or emotion — deficient in acuteness and eloquence, so his psychology is, beside Wagner's, curiously bald and obtuse. One never finds him following the subtler *nuances* of a scene, its finer gradations of mood and temper, its shifting emotional timbre, as does Wagner continually throughout an entire score. Verdi has nothing to compare with such exquisite psychologizing as— to take an example at random — that

crucial passage in the love scene between
Siegmund and Sieglinde in the first act of
"Die Walküre," where Sieglinde suddenly breaks in upon Siegmund's trans-
ports, with her "O Still! lass mich der
Stimme lauschen — mich dünkt, ihren
Klang hört' ich als Kind . . ." and the
orchestra, subsiding in swift obedience to
her mood, ruminates sympathetically.
Verdi apprehends only the surface, the
palpable, aspect of a situation; there is
no modulation (in the emotive sense),
no diversity of accent and emphasis.   I
do not mean to say merely that his
expression is lacking in complexity; if
that were its sole deficiency, one might
very justly rejoin that Verdi aimed at
breadth and totality of view rather
than at close and curious analysis.   My
point is rather this: That he lacks, not
so much complexity as variety; not
simply analytic acuteness, but pene-

trative insight—variety and insight, as
well as vividness, inevitableness, consummate eloquence.

Alphonse Daudet, who wrote of music
with sensitiveness and acumen, somewhere says of Wagner that his "imagination . . . saturates his work to over-
flowing with all the sounds of nature. . . .
The passion between Tristan and Isolde
plunges into the tumult of the ocean
which overwhelms it. . . . One invisible
power raises the waves and the souls by
a single movement . . . water, fire, the
woods, the blossoming and mystic
meadow, become the more powerful
characters." It is in this symbolic use
of the natural world—the use of its
multitudinous sounds and aspects as an
ever-shifting adumbration of the dramatic action—that Wagner stands alone
among tone-painters of the concrete
pictorial. Daudet overshoots the mark,

of course, in supposing that Wagner
ever exalts the external above the
human world—that he ever permits us
to feel that, in his philosophy, "water,
fire, the woods, the blossoming and
mystic meadow" are "the more powerful characters." His winds and waters,
his dawns and clouds and tempests, are
wholly at the service of his dramatic
purposes. He shows us the natural
world as the august and splendid
symbol, the appropriate reflection, of
the emotional life of his dramas. The
tornadic prelude to the third act of
"Siegfried"; the storm that accompanies
the duel between Hunding and Siegmund; the wonderful orchestral transmutation of Isolde's ardors in the earlier
part of the second act of "Tristan,"
and the graphic little seascape at the
opening of the third act, where the
violins, mounting in bleak thirds, paint

at once the dolorously desolate mood
and the pitiless expanse of empty sea—
such things as these have no precise parallel outside of Wagner. Verdi has, it is
true, attempted external tone-painting
(what composer has not?); but one is
hardly under the necessity of ignoring
such original and poetic writing as, for
instance, the brief prelude to the third
act of "Aïda"—in which the essential
mood of nocturnal quietude and mystery
is beautifully achieved — in order con-
scientiously to maintain that the Italian
had neither the German's imaginative
sympathy with, nor his power of
dramatically vivifying, the things of
the natural world. Let me allege, at
random, the orchestral storm with which
"Otello" opens. The music is ef-
fectively conceived; it is adroitly scored;
but it wants just that final heightening
which would make it veracious and

vital—in the sense in which the "Wal-küre" Vorspiel and the overture to "Der Fliegende Holländer" are veracious and vital—and it has only a theatric, not a dramatic significance.

Daudet—to follow him still further—has also this most pregnant observation: "There is everything in Wagner. . . . He made use of the entire human pianoforte and the entire superhuman pianoforte." I doubt if Daudet quite realized what a memorable thing he was saying; but whether or not he was aware of its profounder significance, his remark is deeply and searchingly true. With his usual clarity of vision, he perceived the essential mystic in Wagner; but he failed, nevertheless, to see how com-pletely and fundamentally Wagner's mysticism pervades and informs his art, from "Lohengrin" to "Parsifal," and how absolutely the art is dependent

148

upon a right intuition of the mysticism for its fullest comprehension. The matter is a delicate one to handle; it is so perilously easy, in writing of such things, to decline upon the merely fantastical, and the pitfalls of cant and rhetoric are an ever-present menace to the unwary. Yet I shall venture upon this, speaking as reticently as may be: Daudet's dictum is no mere hyperbolic exaggeration: Wagner compasses not only the human and the natural worlds, but the preternatural—or, as Daudet has it, the "superhuman"—world: the world which we touch, and touch only, by inspiration and intuition. I mean, in plainer phrase, that his music, at its greatest, is compact of subtle spiritual revelations—that it is pervaded, in such things as the "Lohengrin" Vorspiel, Isolde's "Liebestod," and certain parts of "Parsifal," with the purest, most

149

profound, and noblest mysticism that has ever found expression in music. For Wagner, with César Franck, Peter Cornelius, and the mediæval Italians, is of the few genuine musical mystics, and he is the most inspired of these. . . . I suppose it is scarcely necessary to say that he is here in a different world from Verdi. One cannot conceive, without painfully wrenching the imagination, of Verdi as the author of such a thing as the "Liebestod." He was anything but a seer, a visionary, a dreamer of dreams. He never lifted his eyes from the level apparition of the world, nor can one readily believe that he was in the least aware that the world and its human pageant were not all; and even had he lifted his eyes, how much, one wonders, would he have seen?

So we arrive at this summing up of the

expressional scope of these two lyrico-
dramatic poets: Wagner we find to have
made his music, in the deepest and most
widely inclusive sense, an interpretation
of life—of life as emotion, reflecting the
image of the external world, and sur-
charged with spiritual significance. Verdi
we find to be comparatively restricted
in scope and vision; but even within
the obvious limits of his genius, less
perfect a master of purely emotional
expression than Wagner, lacking his
subtlety of exposition and his supremely eloquent utterance. He was not a
path-breaker, and he scaled no heights.
He composed, in those later works
which alone are the important legacy
of his genius, "with his eye on the
object," and he wrought admirably,
nobly, courageously. He has not Wagner's magical felicity, his magnificent
tyranny over the emotions, his lofty

idealism, his universal range. He is scarcely one of the supreme masters; but he is, after Wagner, the most impressive figure in the musico-dramatic art of the nineteenth century.

"PARSIFAL" AND ITS SIG-
NIFICANCE

WHAT rougher prank of ironic fortune
could be imagined than that a work of
art most precious to its creator—the one
of all his achievements which he would
have withheld from common appro-
priation—should suddenly and irreclaim-
ably have been delivered over to the
crowd and to the casual uses of the
paragraphist. It is lamentable enough
when a work of complex and delicate
contrivance is lightly bandied, its subtle
beauty disarrayed; but when that which
has been wrought with lovely artistry
is charged, besides, with a profound and
grave significance, its heedless exploita-

tion can work only perplexity and
distraction. In such an estate to-day is
Wagner's "Parsifal." Its sensational
vicissitudes as an artistic property are
egregiously familiar: known at first hand
a brief while ago only to that incon-
siderable public to whom the arts are of
consequence, and by report to a few
others, this affecting spiritual allegory
has become the topical property of
the man in the street, a profitable
stalking-horse for the pamphleteer.

The thing was, of course, inevitable—
although the consummation was somewhat needlessly abrupt. It could scarcely be expected that an unexampled
masterpiece of musico - dramatic art
should remain indefinitely defiant of
popular curiosity. But if one would
arrive at any sensitive apprehension of
the essential greatness of Wagner's
drama, there is the peril of a fatal con-

fusion in the idle and uninstructed ex-
egesis which has greeted the emergence
of the work into public view; and the
estimates even of those who are wiser
in the ways of art will be found to
be singularly various.   For a few, "Parsifal" marks the summit of Wagner's
accomplishment as a lyric dramatist.
Mr. Ernest Newman, one of the most
acute and authoritative of Wagnerian
critics, finds it "in many ways the most
wonderful and impressive thing ever
done in music"; while at the other end
of the gamut are Mr. James Huneker,
whose scorn of "Parsifal" has been
uttered with exhilarating frankness, and
Mr. John F. Runciman, who devotes
many pages in a volume of essays to
declaring an emphatic and unequivocal
dislike for the master's swan-song.   Nor
is this more than an appraisal of
"Parsifal's" actual artistic value.   It is

when one seeks for a final interpretation of the matter of the work, its poetic and spiritual significance, that confusion and contradiction abound: it is a parable of renunciation, or of redemption; or it is a plea for chastity; or a glorification of sanctity, or of asceticism, or of the beauty of repentance: and, at the end, the seeker after illumination will go again to the work itself and read with steadiness and simplicity of mood, until he understands what Wagner has said, with incomparable eloquence and conviction, in his own luminous and apostolic pages.

A youth, pure in heart, uninstructed in life, comes upon a holy community which is and has long been in distress. One in agony is revealed to him, and high and sacred mysteries are disclosed in his sight. But he is mute, untouched, uncomprehending. Years after, he returns; he has come in close and searing contact with human passion, he has touched life on its most vivid side. Again he comes into the presence of that great grief which before had left him unmoved, and the ancient and splendid mysteries whose meaning had once been veiled to him. Aroused and enlightened, through a clairvoyant intuition of the community of human emotion, he could cry, now, with Anna, in "La Citta Morta": "Vedo, Vedo!" For now he knows, and is prepared to see the Grail in the blinding hour of its illumination.

Is it possible to believe, as Mr. Runciman asks us to believe, that we have here simply a parable of renunciation—that "Parsifal" is a sublimated argument for the "denial of life"? For all that Mr. Runciman, one of the most responsible of contemporary critics, can find to say of Parsifal as a dramatic figure is, that he is set before us merely as one who "deliberately turns from the green world, with its trees and flowers, its dawns and sunsets, its winds and waters, and shuts himself up in a monkery which has a back garden, a pond, and some ducks." The comment has an undeniable vivacity, and its persuasiveness is obvious; but was it quite worth setting down? Mr. Krehbiel, too, finds it possible to say, in his suggestive and scholarly analysis of "Parsifal" in the *Wagnerian Drama* studies, that its central idea, so far as the dramatic spectacle is concerned, is "a glorification of a conception of sanctity which grew out of a monstrous perversion of womanhood." "Of course," he hastens to add, "there is much more in 'Parsifal' than a celebration of the principal feature in mediæval asceticism." But concern-

ing "the dramatic spectacle," too, is
there not much more to be said? Is it
seeing very far into the dramatic substance of the play to find in it nothing
more vital, more immediate, more importunate than the symbolization of a
facile asceticism? Parsifal is found by
Mr. Krehbiel to be endowed "with
scarcely another merit than that which
had become the ideal of monkish
theologians, under the influence of fear-
ful moral depravity and fanatical super-
stition. . . . In the third act, scenes
are borrowed from the life of Christ, and
Parsifal is made to play in them as the
central figure; Kundry anoints the feet
of the knight and dries them with her
hair; Parsifal baptizes Kundry and
absolves her from sin. These acts, and
the resistance of Kundry's seductions
in the magic garden, make up, for the
greater part, the sum of the acts of a

hero in whom the spectator wishes
to see . . . some evidences of the attri-
butes of the heroes of the profoundly
poetical romances from which the subject - matter was drawn." And Mr.
George Moore voices a similar misliking
when, in the brisker manner of his
Ulick Dean, he accounts the sum of
Parsifal's activities to be "the killing
of a swan and the refusal of a kiss."
All of which is, to say the least, insuf-
ficient. Parsifal is, as Mr. Moore has
elsewhere unconsciously suggested, a
subjective hero. It is not the redemption of Amfortas through the conscious
compassion of a guileless simpleton that
is the essential fact. The stage of the
drama is in the heart of Parsifal himself: it is *his* redemption, *his* regeneration that is accomplished. There is the
vital lesson: that none may look upon
the Grail and know it in the splendid

moment of its illumination until he has
first become aware of the vivid reality
of other lives and of the common life
—until, in his brother, he has found
himself. That is the awakening, the
enlightenment: the realizing of our
common humanity, our common des-
tiny. With that intuition and knowl-
edge, and not without,—we are to
understand,—is regeneration attained.
Only so (is the message) can we discover our own selves; and only so may
we sense divine and dæmonic things.

Redemption—objective redemption—
is not, then, the key-note of this searching spiritual fable, as we are so common-
ly told. It is Parsifal, not Amfortas,
who is redeemed: he is the real ben-
eficiary. It is undeniable, of course, that
Wagner was obsessed by the motive of
objective redemption—particularly the
gracious, but spiritually invalid, ideal

which conceives of woman's self-sacri-
ficing love as an instrument of salvation—the informing principle of "Der
Fliegende Holländer," "Tannhäuser,"
and, in part, of "Der Ring des Nibelungen." In his swan-song, the protagonist
is, remarks Mr. W. J. Henderson, a figure
of Christ: "he represents Him when he
is anointed by Gurnemanz, when his feet
are washed by the repentant Kundry,
and when he baptizes her. . . . But more
than all, he surely is the Redeemer when
he touches Amfortas with the holy spear
and bids him

'Be whole, forgiven, and absolved.'

Mr. Henderson's interpretation, so
far as it goes, is sound and just. Wagner,
though, one must remember, had a
singular and most disconcerting habit
of transcending his own elaborately for-
mulated theories, both structural and

ethical. So, as an idealist, he builded, time and again, far better than he knew, uttering often, like Plato's poet, "great and wise things which he himself did not understand." But we who see his work in an objective view are permitted to at-tempt an interpretation.

As "Siegfried" could have been achieved only by a genius whose heart was swept by the sudden tides of youth, so "Parsifal" could have been achieved only by one whose heart had come to know the dreaming wisdom of the seers. That there are many who "would rather be with Cathal of the Woods" than gain the remoter paradise is scarcely surprising; but it is not so, as they have maintained, that in that gain would be heard no more "the earth-sweet ancient song of the blood that is in the veins of youth."

We hear much of the decadence
of Wagner's creative powers as evi-
denced in this final legacy of his inspiration. Recent commentators de-
plore the evil days upon which the
magician of Bayreuth had fallen before his death, and eager scalpels have
laid bare the supposed defects of his
terminal score. Something, indeed,
may be conceded them. It is undeniable that in "Parsifal" Wagner has
not written with the torrential energy,
the superbly prodigal invention, which
went to the creation of his earlier works:
he is not here, unquestionably, so
compelling and forceful, so overwhelming in vitality and climacteric power, as
in the exuberant masterpieces of his artistic prime. But never before, on the
other hand, had this master of illusions
shaped such haunting and subtle symbols of suffering and lamentation, of

sadness and terror, of pity and aspiration. He has written with a more flaming intensity, a more continual inspiration, in "Tristan," in "Götterdämmerung," in "Siegfried," in "Meistersinger"—in the first he is more impassioned, in the second more tragically puissant, lovelier in the third, more immediately human in the fourth. But in no other work are to be found those qualities of grave and poignant tenderness, of august beauty, of essential exaltation, that make the score of "Parsifal" the great and moving thing it is. Not elsewhere in Wagner's writing is there such a theme as that which the commentators have chosen to identify as the "second Herzeleide motive," which appears for the first time when Kundry, in the garden scene of the second act, tells Parsifal of his mother's anguish after he had left her;

nor has he equalled the portentous impressiveness of the chromatic passages of the "changing-scene" in the last act; and how piercing are the phrases with which the "Good Friday" scene closes! Above all, how ineffably lovely is the benign and transfiguring music of the final scene, wherein one may discern a signal of that purification through pity and terror whereby we are put in touch with immortal things.

THE END

CONTENTS

LASAGNA BAKE FOR TWO

PREP: 30 min. \ **TOTAL:** 50 min. \ **MAKES:** 2 servings

---

  2 lasagna noodles, uncooked

  ½ lb. extra-lean ground beef

  ½ cup chopped onions

  1 clove garlic, minced

  1 cup (⅓ of 28-oz. can) undrained canned diced tomatoes

  2 Tbsp. *Philadelphia* Cream Cheese Spread

  4 cups loosely packed baby spinach leaves

  ½ cup *Kraft* Finely Shredded Italian* Five Cheese Blend, divided

1 **Heat** oven to 350°F.

2 **Cook** noodles as directed on package, omitting salt.

3 **Meanwhile,** brown meat with onions and garlic in large nonstick skillet. Add tomatoes and cream cheese spread; cook and stir 2 to 3 min. or until cream cheese is melted and mixture just comes to boil. Add spinach; cook and stir 1 min. Remove from heat. Add ¼ cup shredded cheese; stir until melted.

4 **Drain** noodles. Spoon ⅓ cup spinach mixture into each of 2 (2-cup) ramekins; top with noodle, letting excess noodle extend over rim of ramekin. Top each with ⅓ cup spinach mixture; fold noodle back over dish to cover filling. Repeat until all filling is folded between noodle layers; top with remaining shredded cheese.

5 **Bake** 20 min. or until heated through. Let stand 5 min. before serving.

  *Made with quality cheeses crafted in the USA.

CREAMY TOMATO BAKED RIGATONI

PREP: 20 min. \ **TOTAL:** 55 min. \ **MAKES:** 6 servings, 1¼ cups each

---

    8 oz. (½ of 16-oz. pkg.) rigatoni pasta, uncooked
    2 cups spaghetti sauce
    ½ cup (½ of 8-oz. tub) *Philadelphia* Cream Cheese Spread
    1 cup frozen broccoli florets, thawed
    1 cup frozen cauliflower florets, thawed
    1 cup *Kraft* Shredded Mozzarella Cheese, divided
    ⅓ cup fresh bread crumbs
    2 Tbsp. margarine, melted

1 **Heat** oven to 350°F.

2 **Cook** pasta as directed on package, omitting salt. Meanwhile, microwave spaghetti sauce in large microwaveable bowl on HIGH 1½ to 2 min. or until hot. Add cream cheese spread; stir until well blended. Stir in vegetables and ½ cup mozzarella.

3 **Drain** pasta. Add to vegetable mixture; mix lightly. Spoon into 9-inch square baking dish sprayed with cooking spray. Combine remaining mozzarella, bread crumbs and margarine; sprinkle over pasta mixture.

4 **Bake** 30 to 35 min. or until casserole is heated through and top is golden brown.

HERB & GARLIC MEATBALLS

PREP: 40 min. \ **TOTAL:** 40 min. \ **MAKES:** 4 servings

- **1 lb. extra-lean ground beef**
- **½ cup dry bread crumbs**
- **½ cup (½ of 8-oz. tub)** *Philadelphia* **Chive & Onion Cream Cheese Spread**
- **2 Tbsp. oil**
- **2 cups spaghetti sauce**
- **1 cup water**
- **3 cups hot cooked egg noodles**

1 **Mix** meat, bread crumbs and cream cheese spread until well blended; shape into 24 meatballs, using about 2 Tbsp. for each meatball.

2 **Heat** oil in large nonstick skillet on medium heat. Add meatballs; cook 5 to 6 min. or until evenly browned, turning occasionally. Drain fat from skillet, reserving meatballs in skillet. Add spaghetti sauce and water to skillet; stir to evenly coat meatballs. Simmer on medium-low heat 10 to 15 min. or until meatballs are done (160°F), stirring frequently.

3 **Serve** over noodles.

HOW TO SHAPE MEATBALLS

For evenly sized meatballs, use small ice cream scoop to portion meat mixture for each meatball.

DEEP-DISH CHICKEN POT PIE

PREP: 20 min. \ **TOTAL:** 50 min. \ **MAKES:** 6 servings

---

1 **lb. boneless skinless chicken breasts, cut into 1-inch pieces**

¼ **cup** *Kraft* **Lite Zesty Italian Dressing**

4 **oz. (½ of 8-oz. pkg.)** *Philadelphia* **Neufchâtel Cheese, cubed**

2 **Tbsp. flour**

½ **cup fat-free reduced-sodium chicken broth**

3 **cups frozen mixed vegetables (peas, carrots, corn, green beans), thawed, drained**

1 **ready-to-use refrigerated pie crust (½ of 14.1-oz. pkg.), thawed**

1 **Heat** oven to 375°F.

2 **Cook** chicken in dressing in large skillet on medium heat 2 min. Add Neufchâtel; cook and stir 3 to 5 min. or until melted. Stir in flour until well blended. Add broth and vegetables; stir. Simmer 5 min.

3 **Pour** into deep-dish 10-inch pie plate; cover with pie crust. Seal and flute edge. Cut slits in crust to permit steam to escape.

4 **Bake** 30 min. or until golden brown.

SUBSTITUTE

If a deep-dish pie plate is not available, you can use a 2-qt. round casserole instead.

CREAMY BEEF STROGANOFF

PREP: 50 min. \ **TOTAL:** 50 min. \ **MAKES:** 4 servings

---

1 **beef flank steak (1 lb.)**

1 **Tbsp. margarine**

1 **small onion, chopped**

1 **lb. sliced fresh mushrooms**

2 **bay leaves**

1 **tsp. chopped fresh thyme**

1 **can (14½ oz.) beef broth**

½ **cup (½ of 8-oz. tub) *Philadelphia* Cream Cheese Spread**

¼ **cup chopped fresh parsley**

4 **cups hot cooked egg noodles**

1 Cook steak in large skillet on high heat 2 min. on each side or until browned on both sides. Remove from skillet; cover to keep warm.

2 Add margarine and onions to skillet; cook on medium heat 5 min. or until onions are crisp-tender, stirring occasionally. Stir in mushrooms, bay leaves and thyme; cook 10 min., stirring occasionally. Add broth; bring to boil. Simmer on low heat 3 min. or until slightly thickened. Add cream cheese spread; cook until melted, stirring frequently. Remove and discard bay leaves.

3 Cut steak across the grain into thin slices. Add to skillet; cook 3 to 5 min. or until meat is done. Stir in parsley. Serve over noodles.

VARIATION

Serve over hot cooked rice or mashed potatoes instead of the noodles.

SAUSAGE & PEPPERS LASAGNA

PREP: 30 min. \ **TOTAL:** 1 hour 30 min. \ **MAKES:** 12 servings

---

- ½ lb. Italian sausage
- 1 onion, chopped
- ½ cup <u>each</u> chopped green and red peppers
- 2 pkg. (8 oz. each) *Philadelphia* Cream Cheese, softened
- ½ cup milk
- 2½ cups *Kraft* Shredded Low-Moisture Part-Skim Mozzarella Cheese, divided
- ½ cup *Kraft* Grated Parmesan Cheese, divided
- 1 jar (24 oz.) spaghetti sauce
- ½ cup water
- ½ tsp. dried oregano leaves
- 12 lasagna noodles, cooked

---

1 **Heat** oven to 350°F.

2 **Brown** sausage with vegetables in large skillet. Meanwhile, beat cream cheese and milk in medium bowl with mixer until well blended. Combine mozzarella and Parmesan. Reserve 1½ cups. Add remaining to cream cheese mixture; mix well.

3 **Drain** sausage mixture; return to skillet. Stir in spaghetti sauce, water and oregano. Spread ⅓ of the meat sauce onto bottom of 13×9-inch baking dish; cover with 3 noodles and half the cream cheese mixture. Top with 3 noodles, half the remaining meat sauce and 3 noodles. Cover with layers of remaining cream cheese mixture, noodles, meat sauce and reserved cheese. Cover with foil sprayed with cooking spray.

4 **Bake** 1 hour or until heated through, uncovering after 45 min. Let stand 15 min. before cutting to serve.

VARIATION

Substitute extra-lean ground beef for the sausage and 1 thawed 10-oz. pkg. frozen chopped spinach for the peppers. Squeeze spinach to remove excess liquid before adding to cooked ground beef and onions with the spaghetti sauce and oregano.

CREAMY PASTA PRIMAVERA

PREP: 25 min. \ **TOTAL:** 25 min. \ **MAKES:** 6 servings, 1⅓ cups each

---

  3 cups penne pasta, uncooked

  2 Tbsp. *Kraft* Lite Zesty Italian Dressing

1½ lb. boneless skinless chicken breasts, cut into 1-inch pieces

  2 zucchini, cut into bite-size chunks

1½ cups cut-up fresh asparagus (1-inch lengths)

  1 red pepper, chopped

  1 cup fat-free reduced-sodium chicken broth

  4 oz. (½ of 8-oz. pkg.) *Philadelphia* Neufchâtel Cheese, cubed

  ¼ cup *Kraft* Grated Parmesan Cheese

1 Cook pasta in Dutch oven or large saucepan as directed on package.

2 Meanwhile, heat dressing in large skillet on medium heat. Add chicken and vegetables; cook 10 to 12 min. or until chicken is done, stirring frequently. Add broth and Neufchâtel; cook 2 min. or until Neufchâtel is melted, stirring constantly. Stir in Parmesan.

3 Drain pasta; return to pan. Add chicken mixture; mix lightly. Cook 1 min. or until heated through.

PORK MEDALLIONS ALFREDO

PREP: 20 min. \ **TOTAL:** 20 min. \ **MAKES:** 4 servings, ¼ recipe each

---

- **1 pork tenderloin (1 lb.), cut into ½-inch-thick slices**
- **½ cup (½ of 8-oz. tub) *Philadelphia* Chive & Onion Cream Cheese Spread**
- **⅓ cup fat-free reduced-sodium chicken broth**
- **¼ cup *Kraft* Balsamic Vinaigrette Dressing**
- **1 cup frozen peas**
- **¼ cup *Kraft* Grated Parmesan Cheese**
- **1 Tbsp. lemon juice**
- **4 cups hot cooked egg noodles**
- **2 Tbsp. fresh basil, chopped**

1 **Heat** large heavy nonstick skillet on medium-high heat. Add meat; cook 2 min. on each side or until lightly browned on both sides.

2 **Add** cream cheese spread, broth and dressing; cook and stir 6 min. or until cream cheese is completely melted. Stir in peas, Parmesan and lemon juice; cook until meat is done and sauce is heated through, stirring frequently.

3 **Serve** over noodles; sprinkle with basil.

LINGUINE WITH SILKY MUSHROOM SAUCE

PREP: 20 min. \ **TOTAL:** 20 min. \ **MAKES:** 4 servings, 1¼ cups each

---

- ½ **lb. linguine, uncooked**
- 1 **pkg. (½ lb.) sliced fresh mushrooms**
- ½ **cup fat-free reduced-sodium chicken broth**
- ½ **cup (½ of 8-oz. tub)** *Philadelphia* **Chive & Onion ⅓ Less Fat than Cream Cheese**
- 2 **cups baby spinach leaves**
- 2 **Tbsp.** *Kraft* **Grated Parmesan Cheese**
- **Black pepper**

1 **Cook** pasta as directed on package, omitting salt.

2 **Meanwhile,** heat skillet sprayed with cooking spray on medium-high heat. Add mushrooms; cook and stir 8 min. or until lightly browned. Add broth and reduced-fat cream cheese; cook and stir until cream cheese is melted and sauce is heated through. Add spinach; cook until just wilted, stirring frequently.

3 **Drain** pasta; toss with sauce. Sprinkle with Parmesan cheese and pepper.

SHORTCUT

Packaged sliced fresh mushrooms are available in the produce department of your grocery store.

FISH IN ROASTED RED PEPPER SAUCE

PREP: 30 min. \ **TOTAL:** 30 min. \ **MAKES:** 4 servings

- 4 **white fish fillets, such as tilapia or cod (1 lb.)**
- ¼ **cup flour**
- ¼ **cup *Kraft* Zesty Italian Dressing**
- ½ **cup sliced onions**
- 2 **oz. (¼ of 8-oz. pkg.) *Philadelphia* Cream Cheese, softened**
- ¼ **cup roasted fresh red peppers**
- ¼ **cup chicken broth**
- 1 **clove garlic**
- 2 **Tbsp. chopped fresh cilantro**

1 **Coat** both sides of fish fillets with flour. Heat dressing in large skillet on medium-high heat. Add onions; cook and stir 5 min. or until crisp-tender. Add fish; cook 5 to 7 min. on each side or until fish flakes easily with fork.

2 **Meanwhile,** blend cream cheese, red peppers, broth and garlic in blender until smooth; pour into saucepan. Bring to boil on medium-high heat, stirring frequently; simmer on low heat 5 min., stirring occasionally.

3 **Serve** fish topped with cream cheese sauce and cilantro.

SUBSTITUTE

Substitute jarred roasted red peppers or roasted poblano peppers for the roasted fresh red peppers.

CURRY WITH PORK & PEPPERS

PREP: 30 min. \ **TOTAL:** 30 min. \ **MAKES:** 4 servings, 1¼ cups each

---

- **1 lb. pork tenderloin, cut into 1-inch pieces**
- **1 onion, cut into 1-inch pieces**
- **1 red pepper, cut into 1-inch pieces**
- **1 green pepper, cut into 1-inch pieces**
- **½ cup (½ of 8-oz. tub) *Philadelphia* Cream Cheese Spread**
- **1 Tbsp. Thai yellow curry paste**
- **½ cup coconut milk**
- **½ cup water**
- **2 cups hot cooked long-grain white rice**

1 **Heat** large skillet sprayed with cooking spray on medium-high heat. Add meat; cook and stir 4 min. or until evenly browned. Add vegetables; cook 4 to 6 min. or until vegetables are crisp-tender, stirring constantly.

2 **Add** cream cheese spread, curry paste, coconut milk and water; cook until cream cheese is melted, stirring constantly. Bring just to boil; simmer on medium-low heat 8 to 10 min. or until meat is done, stirring frequently.

3 **Serve** with rice.

SPECIAL EXTRA

Top with ¼ cup chopped fresh cilantro or toasted *Baker's Angel Flake* Coconut just before serving.

MOZZARELLA-STUFFED CHICKEN BREASTS

PREP: 20 min. \ **TOTAL:** 50 min. \ **MAKES:** 4 servings, 1 stuffed chicken breast each

---

2 oz. (¼ of 8-oz. pkg.) *Philadelphia* Neufchâtel Cheese, softened

¼ cup finely chopped green peppers

½ tsp. dried oregano leaves

¼ tsp. garlic salt

1 cup *Kraft* Shredded Mozzarella Cheese, divided

4 small boneless skinless chicken breast halves (about 1 lb.), pounded to ¼-inch thickness

1 cup spaghetti sauce

1 **Heat** oven to 400°F.

2 **Mix** first 4 ingredients until well blended; stir in ½ cup mozzarella.

3 **Place** chicken, top-sides down, on work surface; spread with cheese mixture. Starting at one short end, tightly roll up each breast; place, seam-side down, in 8-inch square baking dish sprayed with cooking spray. Spoon spaghetti sauce over chicken; cover.

4 **Bake** 30 min. or until chicken is done (165°F). Sprinkle with remaining mozzarella; bake, uncovered, 3 to 5 min. or until melted.

GREEK CHICKEN WITH TZATZIKI SAUCE

PREP: 15 min. \ **TOTAL:** 45 min. \ **MAKES:** 4 servings

½ cup (½ of 8-oz. tub) *Philadelphia* Cream Cheese Spread

2 Tbsp. chopped fresh dill

6 Tbsp. milk

1 Tbsp. lemon juice

1 green onion, chopped

1 clove garlic, minced

1 lb. boneless skinless chicken breasts, cut into 1-inch pieces

¼ cup finely chopped English cucumbers

1 **Whisk** first 6 ingredients until well blended. Pour half over chicken in medium bowl; stir to evenly coat. Stir cucumbers into remaining sauce. Refrigerate both 20 min.

2 **Heat** grill to medium-high heat. Remove chicken from marinade; discard marinade. Thread chicken onto 8 skewers. Grill 8 to 10 min. or until chicken is done, turning occasionally.

3 **Serve** with tzatziki sauce.

SERVING SUGGESTION

Serve with hot cooked whole grains and your favorite vegetables.

CREAMY SHRIMP LINGUINE

PREP: 25 min. \ **TOTAL:** 25 min. \ **MAKES:** 4 servings, 1½ cups each

---

8 oz. linguine, uncooked

1 Tbsp. oil

1 lb. uncooked deveined peeled large shrimp

2 cloves garlic, minced

½ cup (½ of 8-oz. tub) *Philadelphia* Cream Cheese Spread

2 Tbsp. chopped fresh dill

¾ cup fat-free reduced-sodium chicken broth

1 Tbsp. lemon zest

2 cups snow peas, halved

1 cup cherry tomatoes, halved

1 **Cook** pasta as directed on package, omitting salt.

2 **Meanwhile,** heat oil in large nonstick skillet on medium-high heat. Add shrimp and garlic; cook and stir 3 to 5 min. or until shrimp turn pink. Remove from heat; cover to keep warm.

3 **Add** cream cheese spread, dill, broth and zest; cook and stir 2 to 3 min. or until cream cheese is melted and sauce is well blended. Add shrimp, snow peas and tomatoes; cook and stir 3 min. or until heated through.

4 **Drain** pasta. Add to shrimp mixture; toss to coat.